# MICHAEL GRAVES

# MICHAEL GRAVES

## BUILDINGS AND PROJECTS
## 1995–2003

EDITED BY KAREN NICHOLS
ESSAY BY FRANCISCO SANIN

*RIZZOLI* NEW YORK

# Acknowledgments

First published in the United States of America in 2003 by
RIZZOLI INTERNATIONAL PUBLICATIONS, INC.
300 Park Avenue South
New York, NY 10010

*Frontispiece: Archaic Landscape, painting by Michael Graves*

Distributed to the United States trade by
St. Martin's Press, New York

2003 2004 2005 2006 2007 / 10 9 8 7 6 5 4 3 2 1

Printed and bound in China
Designed by Abigail Sturges

ISBN: 0-8478-2652-X (HC)
ISBN: 0-8478-2569-8 (PB)

Library of Congress Catalog Control Number: 2003104772

This monograph on the buildings and projects designed by
Michael Graves & Associates is the fourth volume in a series
documenting the chronology of our architectural practice. As
a principal of the firm and editor of this book, I would like to
acknowledge the collaborative efforts of many people.
Special thanks go to Stephen Case and David Morton of
Rizzoli for their continued support and guidance, and to
Abigail Sturges and her staff for graphic design services.
Francisco Sanin, a long-time colleague and friend, con-
tributed the essay.

Many staff members of Michael Graves & Associates played
essential roles in preparing and assembling the photographs,
drawings and text. Michael Graves and the four principals
who are studio heads—Patrick Burke, John Diebboll, Gary
Lapera and Tom Rowe—provided ongoing advice and guidance regarding the contents. Courtney Havran, the firm's
images librarian, took responsibility for organizing all of the
artwork. Marek Bulaj was responsible for in-house photography, and Caroline Hancock assisted with the text. Andrew
Merz contributed to the early organization of the book.

The considerable effort to track down and assemble hundreds
of project drawings was led by two associates, Craig Babe and
Mark Proicou. They were most recently assisted by numerous
staff members including, among others, Jacqueline Teo,
Ludwing Vaca, Stephanie Rigolot, Maria Ruiz, Brian
Ambroziak, Matt Ligas and Emily Estes.

Karen Nichols, FAIA
Princeton, New Jersey
2003

# Contents

# The Language of Michael Graves

*Francisco Sanin*

*Archaic Landscape*

Over the last three decades the work of Michael Graves has maintained a consistency and a commitment to an idea that very few architects have. In the face of changing movements, fashions and conditions, he has continued to pursue the idea of an architectural language and to explore its transformation and boundaries. In fact, the essay entitled "A Case for Figurative Architecture," which he wrote for his first Rizzoli monograph covering the years 1966–1981, could still be read as an introduction to the work published in this, the fourth volume in the series. A basic premise of that article is his statement that "it is crucial that we re-establish the thematic associations invented by our culture in order to allow the culture of architecture to represent the mythic and ritual aspirations of society." It was his contention then, as it is today, that only when architecture is engaged as a language and a figurative art can it maintain its relevance to society.

It is important to note that the argument developed in that article was framed not only in cultural terms but also, most interestingly, in terms of the potential for the figurative characteristics of architecture to be a source of invention and a stimulus for the architectural imagination. This it seems has been the force that has driven Graves' work: a commitment to an architecture that can communicate through its figurative qualities, and a corresponding commitment to explore the boundaries or limits of such a proposition. In the introduction to Graves' second monograph covering the years 1982–1989, Robert Maxwell discussed Graves' fascination with both rules and transgression, with the structures of language as a necessary foil for his own creativity: "Graves' dilemma is a tough one: in a time when all resolutions are considered provisional, he has to fight as hard to establish the rule system that will permit closure as he must fight to put the rules into question by transgressing them."

Graves' article on figurative architecture was a very influential text for a whole generation of architects who were looking for an alternative to what they saw as the limitations of modern architecture, specifically the incapacity to respond to new conditions of society and to convey meaning. Much has happened in architecture since the 1960s and 1970s when the debate focused on the need, and the potential, to explore the linguistic dimensions of architecture. As a professor at Princeton University (Graves recently retired after 39 years of teaching), he has been both a protagonist in and a witness to the major critical debates of the last four decades. It is well known that in the 1970s and 1980s Princeton was the center of some of the most intense debates about modernism and postmodernism, with the presence of theorists such as

Robert Maxwell, Alan Colquhoun and Anthony Vidler, among others. During that time, Graves' work at the university developed, if not in an atmosphere of complete agreement and theoretical alliances, at least in an atmosphere of common understanding of the basic references and boundaries of the discourse. By the late 1980s and early 1990s, the panorama had changed with the presence of theorists such as Mark Wigley and Beatriz Colomina. Princeton had become a center of debate on deconstructivist theory. Despite this changing context, Graves maintained his own line of work and inquiry. One may wonder if being in the middle of a debate that was quite distant from his own led him to become even more radicalized in his position. As described by Janet Abrams in her essay in Graves' third monograph dated 1990–1994, Graves saw himself becoming more of a radical by staying his course at a time when architectural debate was moving away from issues of language, meaning and representation.

His interest in an architecture that communicates and is thus accessible to the popular imagination led him further away from the debates not only in Princeton but also in the mainstream of academia. He seems to have focused instead on his architectural practice and his growing interest in product design, works that have brought him closer and closer to a mass audience. This desire to engage in a direct manner with popular culture has led to some of his most controversial designs, such as those for the Walt Disney Company, works that made some question how far one can go in this direction before the search for meaning becomes a rhetorical act. While admitting the challenges posed by the required "theming" of those projects, Graves saw the effect of his language another way: "It was like being a playwright who needed to master the difficulties of both tragedy and comedy."

Whatever the forum, Graves' work has maintained a lifelong commitment to the values of architecture as a language, a patient exploration of the potential and limits of that language. While he has not written much about his own architecture in recent times, his body of work itself reveals a continuous process of research and speculation.

Graves draws and paints. These are the tools of his trade and the methods of his research. Much has been written about his early experimentation with cubist themes and their relation to his building design strategies, both the organization of plans and the expression of building facades. His article, "The Necessity for Drawing: Tangible Speculation," published in *A.D. Magazine* in 1978, established drawing as the basis for

*Pura-Williams Residence preliminary model*

*Topeka Library entrance*

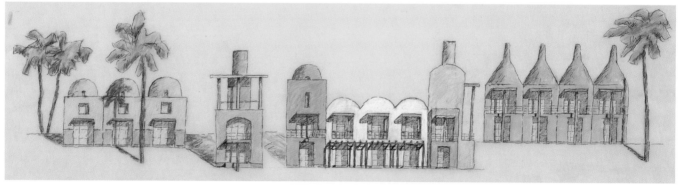

*El Gouna hotels character studies*

experimentation as well as documentation. Since then, painting has become not only his favorite form of expression but also the very site where he initially explores architectural and spatial ideas and, furthermore, the site where one can see them emerge in a more distilled form. Indeed, one can follow the development of his ideas from his early explorations in cubism, collage and transparency, to his subsequent fascination with Italian landscapes, and more recently to paintings in which one can see the emergence of new themes, themes that are more abstract and laconic, even enigmatic. These paintings are imaginary landscapes populated by objects that look familiar yet distant, shapes without specific scale or reference, strangely material and present and yet abstract. They remain within the language, and yet they do not convey a specific meaning other than their own presence.

One can see some of these qualities in several of his recent projects, a move away from his characteristic emphasis on the composition of plans and facades to a more objectlike, almost typological, approach. In a project such as the Pura-Williams

house of 1994, the composition is a collection (not really a collage) of architectural types; we recognize the vault, the cone, the cube in ways that remind one of Piero Ligorio's drawings of ancient Rome (which are among Graves' favorite references). However, the types have been transformed. Through shifts in scale and proportion and through the manipulation of elements such as windows and canopies, the forms are read in different and unexpected ways. Take for example, the canopies at the end of the office wing—one canopy on top of the other, too thin to be useful, and the column that supports them, too thick to be merely structural. Graves is playing a game with the language. At one moment the forms appear familiar, yet upon a closer look their condition is no longer so, creating a sort of delayed meaning that both puzzles and stimulates the imagination. One can say the same about the entrance "drum" of the library in Topeka and about the many pavilions of the resorts in El Gouna and Taba Heights, Egypt, in which the very nature of the program seems to have allowed Graves the space to explore all kinds of architectural inventions. Most of those buildings, which

*El Gouna hotels details*

are groups of guestrooms, utilize traditional local construction techniques featuring brick vaults, domes and arches. Graves uses these buildings as a point of departure to engage in a process of elaboration and invention that leads to some surprising results. While the individual pavilions offer a great variety of forms and transformations, the overall plan remains more in the tradition of previous projects in which the main concern is order and hierarchy, in which the plan provides a clarity that stabilizes the diversity of the three-dimensional compositions. The question remains as to what it means to use a local typology without making reference to the spatial fabric where it traditionally existed.

There are many other trends in Graves' current work, too numerous to mention here. Graves attributes this variety to his exploration of architectural character, and not to stylistic interest. Character, for him, is a way of creating and conveying meaning based on a figurative language. "Whether the architecture subliminally describes its function (for example, a civic building as opposed to a house) or explicitly responds

to its physical or cultural context, it relies on the use of familiar elements in the belief that people make natural associations with forms, colors and materials." Thus, the themes developed in the work demonstrate a broad range, from the vernacular to the neoclassical, from the figurative to the abstract. Compare for example, a library in the specific neo-Georgian context of Alexandria, Virginia to the more elaborate speculations in the Cotton Bay and Canary Islands resorts. In the Cotton Bay resort, the small pavilions seem to use the local vernacular as a point of departure. Given their relatively small scale, they are able to make reference to traditional construction methods and materials, something that is harder to do in the main hotel building given its size and scale. This exploration of the vernacular has limits when applied to a larger scale, since the specificity of the individual elements creates an uneasy tension when stretched over a more extensive composition.

In other projects such as St. Mary's Church in Florida, the simple and somewhat abstract forms possess a clarity and

*Resort Hotel at Cotton Bay bar and restaurant*

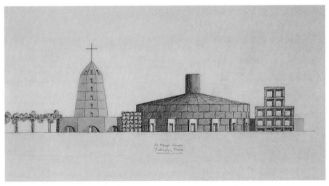

*St. Mary's Church south elevation*

power almost devoid of any tectonic or material quality—at least in the drawings and photographs—of scale. The themes are form, space, light and color. Compare this project to the student housing at Rice University, where the facades are conceived as a manipulation of the traditional and tangible elements of materials and construction—the frame, the horizontal banding, the brick infill and so on. The "expected" elements of the facade as construction are present but their proportions have been changed; the horizontal elements are so compressed that they become "too thin," and the bay windows are supported by one single column that gives them a strange figural condition. Graves seems to be concerned not with the tectonic but with the transformation of the elements of construction into a language that sets up a new system of relationships and proportions. Although he uses a traditional vocabulary of architectural elements, his interest is not to adopt the classical language of architecture in the strictest sense. Instead, he says, "I look at the root of the word 'classical' as it conveys the sense of classification, or hierarchical organization. My architectural language may classify the parts of a composition, such as the base, body and head of a tripartite facade or even a column, but it avoids the specific stylistic references." Thus, Graves continues to regard language itself as a source of invention and as a means to exercise his artistic imagination.

It is Graves' ability to continue to explore and expand the potential and the limits of the traditional language of architecture that sets his work apart from the rest. Most proponents of classical architecture seem to be interested in the canons and rules and in reducing the language to common denominators, reduced so it can be imitated. In contrast, Graves is constantly expanding his vocabulary. At a time when most architects have abandoned the idea of traditional architecture as a language, Graves has been left with the whole field to himself, and, like a child in an enormous playground, he is thoroughly enjoying the game.

Graves' interest in the figurative dimension of architecture has to do with its ability to communicate, to be understood by the "public," both in terms of the language and in terms of the space where architecture makes its presence. His projects continue to relate to ideas of public space based on known types: the square, the portico, the courtyard and the spatial sequence between inside and outside. In addition to exploring the figurative aspect of buildings, he continues to be interested in the potential figural quality of space defined by the building facades that surround it.

Of course, one can ask if it is still possible today to speak of common public space in a world wherein the logic is to reinvent—if not the languages—at least the systems of signification, so as to allow for a perpetual system of consumption. In these systems it is no longer possible to find consensus about what is good or bad, right or wrong. In a world of constant change and at a moment in history when information and communication tend to flow along non-material axes, is there still a role for a view that poses architecture as a cultural artifact capable of creating the conditions for public space? Clearly Graves thinks there should be. To put it another way, his position, if not a critique or a resistant stance, demonstrates his interest in exploring an alternative. A short anecdote may illustrate this point. Once, in a discussion with a colleague at Princeton, Graves questioned the fact that his colleague, a proponent of a different and completely non-traditional view of architecture, surrounded himself with traditional artifacts. I believe the example had to do with some English leather couches. The colleague's response was something like, "…but Michael, do you still believe in the continuity between life and art?" Graves responded, "Of course, an architect's art affects someone else's life." Whether one agrees with Graves' position or even shares his optimism, one has to respect the integrity and sincerity of his commitment.

Graves has been one of the major protagonists in the history of architecture in the last decades, as is attested by many publications and the significant awards he has received, including the American Institute of Architects Gold Medal and the National Medal of Arts, a presidential award. His work continues to evolve and change and to ask questions. Even at a time when some have declared what they call "the end of the semiotic nightmare," work like that of Graves argues that issues of representation are not so easily brushed aside. His work continues to ask questions about architecture in general and to test the limits of his own propositions in particular.

One may wish for Graves to write about his own work and ideas about architecture as he did in the early days when he would also talk about his design process, particularly the role of drawing as a form of speculation. His monographs are elegant and eloquent displays of his work, yet one still wishes there would be more of an attempt to make explicit both the ideas and the process that generates them. It may be just that in the current climate of critical debate about architecture, it is not enough to let the buildings speak for themselves. The cultural landscape has changed dramatically; it is now necessary to have a way to gain access to the development of ideas. Since Graves' work continues to be provocative and

*Martel College student residence wing*

rich in possibilities, a look inside the process can only help provoke a wider discussion. In the words of Robert Maxwell, in the essay mentioned above, "Viewed in this way, the work of Michael Graves takes on the character of play (as with any artist), a continual experimenting with his preferred materials and the opportunities that come to hand. That is not to deny its underlying seriousness. But it does enable us to assert its experimental nature and, in this sense to recognize that he is as much entitled to his space as any other artist, of whatever ideological color. And perhaps recognize also that he is doing useful work for the rest of us."

Graves' early decision to look for a direct engagement with popular culture has clearly paid off. By now he has become an established figure. His buildings are found in all corners of the world, from Europe to China, from Japan to Egypt, and in many cities across America, and his product designs have made him a household name throughout the world. It may be that recent changes in architectural debate are creating a climate in which it would be possible to examine his work in an objective way. At a time when the architectural landscape is going through major transformations, becoming more complex and fluid, it is time to drop the various "isms" that have been attached to Graves' work, and thus to have a more serious and critical discussion of the important contributions made to the discipline of architecture by the long career of this committed and very talented architect.

*Syracuse–Seoul, July 2003*

# List of Building and Projects

International Finance
Corporation Headquarters

*Washington, D.C., 1992*

*Lobby*

The headquarters of the World Bank Group's International Finance Corporation is located on a triangular site on Pennsylvania Avenue at Washington Circle. The architectural design of the 12-story building provides a fresh approach to classical organization and detailing within the context of traditional Washington. Several pavilions are pulled forward from the body of building along Pennsylvania Avenue, which helps break down the scale of the 600-foot-long facade and provides opportunities to plan numerous corner offices. A distinctive cylindrical belvedere marks the corner of the site at Washington Circle.

In addition to offices, the program for this 1.1-million-square-foot building includes common facilities such as a conference and training center, multipurpose auditorium, library, cafeteria and dining rooms. The full-height atrium with its expansive skylight allows natural light into the center of the building and serves as a focal point for orientation and circulation.

*Reception*

*Facing page: Dining room*

*Auditorium*

1 Lobby
2 Atrium
3 Credit union
4 Meeting/dining room
5 Travel office
6 Open to below
7 Library

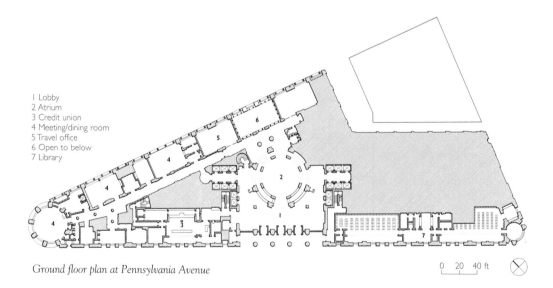

*Ground floor plan at Pennsylvania Avenue*

0  20  40 ft

# Arts and Sciences Building
# Richard Stockton College

*Pomona, New Jersey, 1992*

The 37,000-square-foot Arts and Sciences Building at Richard Stockton College in the Pine Barrens of New Jersey establishes a gateway to the linked modern buildings of the campus developed in the 1970s. The entrance, a brick and cast stone portico, is located on axis with the concourse of the original buildings. A lecture hall with campus-wide usage is located on one side of the entrance. On the other side, a semi-detached art gallery was designed for future construction.

The building is arranged in a U-shaped configuration around a central, inward-facing courtyard. Faculty offices, study rooms and common areas face the courtyard, and classrooms, laboratories and studios face outward. The courtyard is articulated with closely spaced columns of green glazed brick reminiscent of the surrounding pine forests. The exterior of the building is clad in terra cotta, ochre and blue-green brick and cast stone, reflecting the colors of the sandy soil, indigenous vegetation and waterways of the Pine Barrens.

*Courtyard*

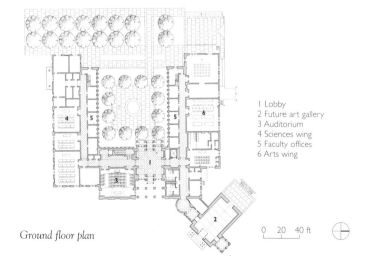

1 Lobby
2 Future art gallery
3 Auditorium
4 Sciences wing
5 Faculty offices
6 Arts wing

*Ground floor plan*

0    20    40 ft

Auditorium

Entrance facade

## Indianapolis Art Center
*Indianapolis, Indiana, 1992*

*Entrance facade*

The Indianapolis Art Center contains studios for painting, sculpture, ceramics, photography and printmaking, an art gallery for changing exhibits, a 250-seat auditorium, a library, a gift shop and administrative offices. Site constraints limited the building's footprint to a long narrow bar of approximately 40,000 square feet and restricted the height to one story. Variations in window types help offset the effect of the length of the primary facades. The entrance and garden porticoes establish an axis through the building aligned with the termination of Ferguson Street, which links the Art Center with Broadripple Village five blocks away. The library is located in an octagonal pavilion facing the garden. The studios face north and open directly onto gardens along the White River, creating literal and figurative links between art and nature. Subsequent projects at the Indianapolis Art Center include the development of the gardens as a sensory art park for sculpture exhibitions and special events.

1 Gallery
2 Library
3 Auditorium
4 Studios

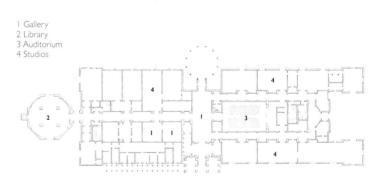

Ground floor plan

0   20   40 ft

Library

## Astrid Park Plaza Hotel

*Antwerp, Belgium, 1992*

*View from lounge toward train station*

The mixed-use building in which the Astrid Park Plaza Hotel is located occupies an important urban site at the north end of Astrid Square facing Antwerp's monumental Beaux-Arts train station. In addition to the 240-room hotel, the building contains commercial office space, a conference center, a shopping center, restaurants and bars, underground parking and an entrance to the subterranean city-wide Metro system.

The massing, character and materials of the building reflect the eclectic nature of the immediate context and Antwerp in general. The architecture of this historic city is characterized by the richness of building facades that provide continuous streetwalls defining the public squares as outdoor rooms. Likewise, the frontal nature of the Astrid Park Plaza Hotel creates a sense of closure for Astrid Square and complements the massing of the train station. The main facade consists of a central section flanked by two narrow towers. A lower, cylindrical tower adjoining the west wall of the hotel contains retail shops and specialized hotel functions.

*South facade facing Astrid Square*

*Ground floor plan*

*Second floor plan*

1 Hotel lobby
2 Hotel lounge
3 Retail
4 Business center lobby
5 Metro entrance
6 Garage entrance
7 Restaurant
8 Prefunction
9 Meeting room
10 Banquet hall

0  5  10 m

*Facing page: Banquet hall*

Restaurant

*Typical guestroom*

# Castalia
# Ministries of Health, Welfare and Sport

*The Hague, Netherlands, 1993*

In the early 1990s, the architect Rob Krier prepared a mixed-use master plan for an area of The Hague called de Resident, which proposed a combination of new infill construction and renovation of existing buildings. Among the existing buildings was a 1950s jack-slab building that had been stripped of its failing facade and core and reduced to its structural system. Michael Graves & Associates was commissioned to redesign this building for the headquarters of the Ministries of Health, Welfare and Sport.

The building, known as Castalia, was expanded to 25 stories and 29,000 square meters in area. The design strategy reconciles the small scale of existing low-rise housing with the larger scale of surrounding medium- and high-rise office buildings. Its articulation as "twin towers" separated by protruding bay windows of glazed brick reinforces a new vertical reading. The dual towers also signified the initial intention that two ministries would occupy the building. The distinctive profile on the city skyline is reminiscent of the shape of typical Dutch steeply gabled roofs. While accommodating the constraints of the existing structure, the planar brick facades feature gridded window patterns characteristic of local traditional architecture although at a much larger scale.

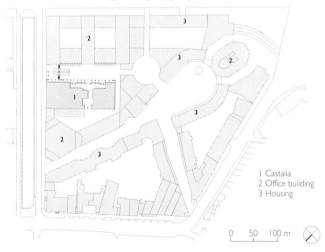

*de Resident site with existing building to right of center*

1 Castalia
2 Office building
3 Housing

0    50    100 m

*Site plan*

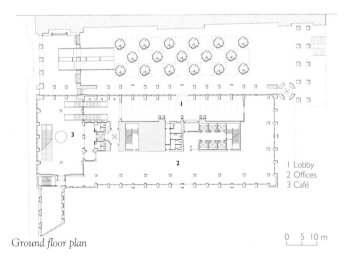

1 Lobby
2 Offices
3 Café

0    5   10 m

*Ground floor plan*

City view

*Lobby*

## Nexus Momochi
## Residential Tower

*Fukuoka, Japan, 1993*

View from the bay

Lobby

For the 1989 Asian-Pacific Exposition, the city of Fukuoka reclaimed a large portion of its bayside waterfront as a new residential district, which included a five-story apartment building designed by Michael Graves & Associates. Several years later, the firm was commissioned to design a 27-story luxury apartment tower at the end of the axis established by that first building. The tower, the tallest building in the area, occupies one of the most prestigious sites in this internationally acclaimed district. The building's exterior is composed as a slender, ochre-colored frame of precast concrete applied over a glass curtain wall. The layered yet transparent quality of the facade gives the tower a luminous presence when seen from the water, appearing as an abstract version of a lighthouse. The facade's generous fenestration also provides the apartments with spectacular waterfront views.

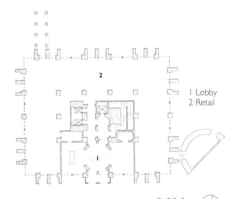

1 Lobby
2 Retail

Ground floor plan

0 2.5 5 m

Taiwan National Museum
of Pre-History

*Taitung City, Taiwan, 1993*

Located near an important Neolithic archaeological site at Peinan on Taiwan's scenic Eastern coast, the National Museum of Pre-history is dedicated to the study, preservation and public exhibition of artifacts from the site, as well as materials from other prehistoric Austronesian cultures. The campus provides extensive indoor and outdoor visitor facilities, including interpretive exhibits that tell the story of man's evolving relationship with nature. The program for the 425,000-square-foot main building includes flexible exhibit galleries, a 200-seat theater, an international conference center, a research library, offices, curatorial laboratories and archival storage.

Major public programmatic elements are expressed as individual pavilions organized around a monumental courtyard. This outdoor space, the focal point of the complex, is designed for ceremonial performances and other public events. The campus is landscaped as a park, using the natural landforms and vegetation to evoke the feeling of prehistoric sites.

*Northwest elevation*

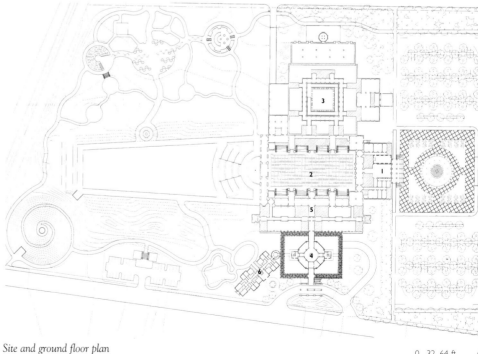

1 Visitor entrance
2 Mountain Square exhibit
3 Gallery
4 Administration entrance
5 Administrative offices
6 Academic research center

*Site and ground floor plan*

0  32  64 ft

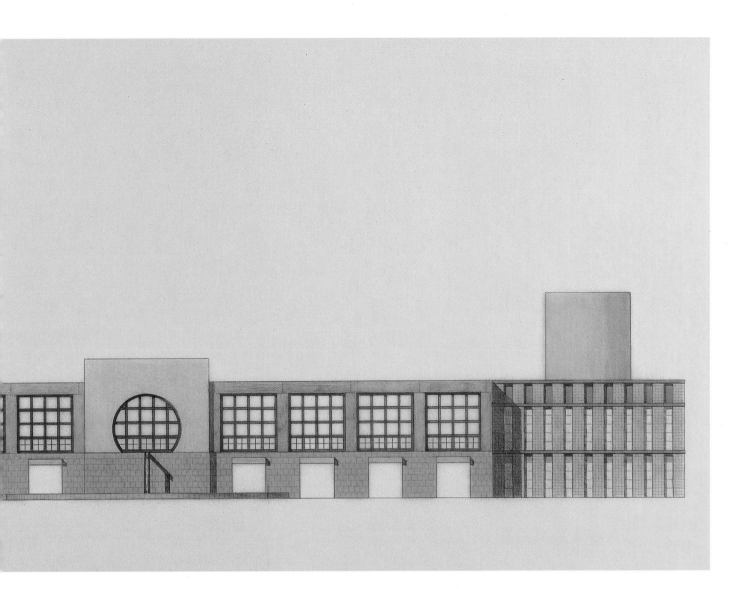

*Entrance pavilion elevation*

*View from the north*

*Exhibit*

# United States Post Office

*Celebration, Florida, 1993*

*View from the Town Square*

The Post Office, located adjacent to Town Hall in the new community of Celebration, Florida, is composed in two simple parts: a rotunda that serves as the public entrance, and a rectangular block with an open-air loggia where mailboxes are located. The character of the Post Office respects the traditions of the building type as well as the prevailing architecture of the region. The rotunda announces this small building's public presence while the form of the loggia and the materials and colors of the building are typical of small-scale architecture found throughout Florida.

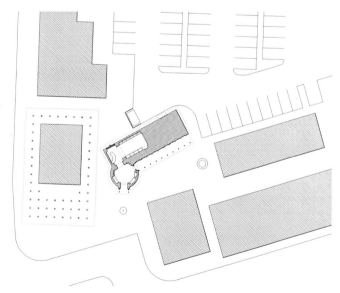

*Site and ground floor plan*

0  20  40 ft

# Disney's Garden Pavilions

*Orlando, Florida, 1994*

*View from the Walt Disney World® Dolphin Hotel*

Two linked garden pavilions — the Sorcerer's Apprentice Pavilion and Dancing Hippos Pavilion — comprise a large-scale outdoor facility for special events, receptions and parties, located on the grounds of the Walt Disney World® Dolphin Hotel and Walt Disney World® Swan Hotel near Orlando, Florida. The covered but open-air spaces are supported by internal kitchen and restroom facilities. A large terrace with a stage adjoins them. Although the pavilions are permanent structures, the roofs have the character of tents so as to reinforce the temporary, festive nature of the activities taking place in the garden.

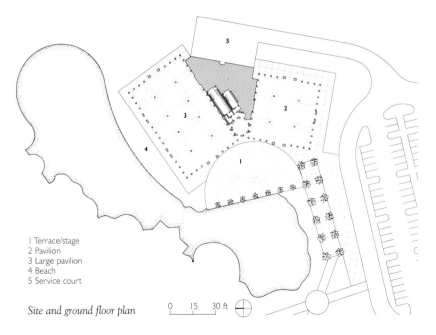

1 Terrace/stage
2 Pavilion
3 Large pavilion
4 Beach
5 Service court

*Site and ground floor plan*   0   15   30 ft

**1500 Ocean Drive**

*Miami Beach, Florida, 1994*

Cartoon for mural by Michael Graves

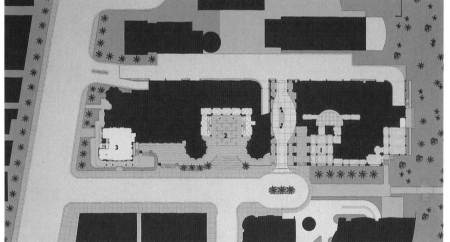

Site plan

0   50   100 ft

The residential condominiums at 1500 Ocean Drive and the adjoining retail center, Ocean Steps, are located at the intersection of 15th Street and Ocean Drive in South Beach. The project's articulation, colors and detailing respect the scale and character of the context, which includes the adjacent famous Art Deco district and several contemporary apartment buildings.

The 15-story, 111-unit condominium building is oriented toward the ocean. Its beachfront cylindrical tower, evocative of a coastal beacon, offers panoramic views of the surroundings. Retail, restaurant and office spaces are contained in the former Bancroft Hotel, an adjacent historic Art Deco building which was renovated for retail and office use. A U-shaped retail courtyard at the visual terminus of Ocean Drive links the condominiums and the Bancroft Hotel.

1 Condominium building entrance
2 Ocean Steps retail center
3 Former Bancroft Hotel

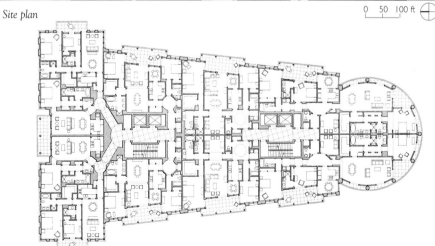

Typical condominium floor plan

0   20   40 ft

## One Port Center

*Camden, New Jersey, 1994*

One Port Center, the headquarters of the Delaware River Port Authority of New Jersey and Pennsylvania, is a cornerstone of the redevelopment of Camden, New Jersey. The L-shaped site flanks an existing parking garage. The master plan for the area accommodates a future companion building on the other side of the parking garage. Overlooking the Delaware River, the site offers spectacular views toward Philadelphia.

The 176,000-square-foot, 11-story building contains retail shops and a restaurant at the base, four floors of leased office space, and six floors of offices for the Port Authority. The executive offices and boardroom are located on the top floor of the building behind three-story yellow aluminum composite columns. The blue and white glazed brick used at the lower level makes reference to the building's waterfront location.

*Boardroom*

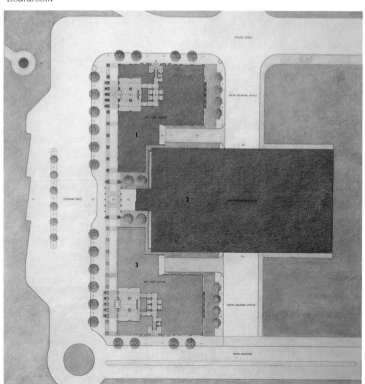

*Site plan with current and future buildings*

0  20  40 ft

1 One Port Center
2 Parking garage
3 Future building

House at Coolidge Point

*Manchester-by-the-Sea,*
*Massachusetts, 1994*

This single-family house is located on a bluff along the rocky New England coast, approximately 60 feet from the Atlantic Ocean. In response to both program and site, individual pavilions — a residence, an office, guest quarters, swimming pool, pool house and garden elements — are given their own identities. The casual nature of the composition in plan is reminiscent of New England compounds developed over time.

Each pavilion in the composition contains a separate function. The living and dining rooms anchor the composition, with other pavilions pinwheeling off this central block. The easternmost pavilion contains a library in a rotunda-like form. Internally, it acts as a hinge connecting the office, guest quarters, and the winter garden and pool. Externally, it acts as a marker, reminiscent of the lighthouses that characterize the region. Two courtyards, one forming the entry and the other facing the water, along with a variety of framed views, establish reciprocal relationships between the building and the landscape.

*Porch overlooking the ocean*

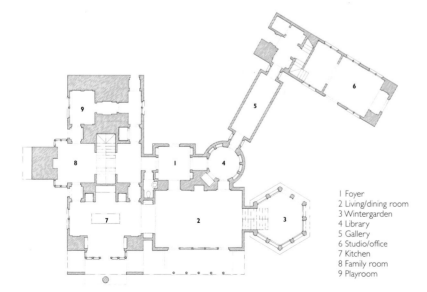

1 Foyer
2 Living/dining room
3 Wintergarden
4 Library
5 Gallery
6 Studio/office
7 Kitchen
8 Family room
9 Playroom

*Ground floor plan*

0    10    20 ft

*Kitchen*

*Library*

**Miramar Resort Hotel**
*El Gouna, Egypt, 1995*

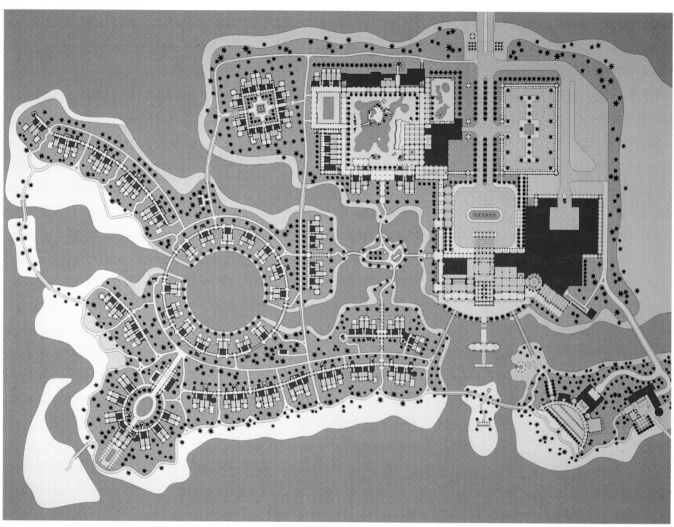

*Site and ground floor plan*

0   25   50 ft

The Sheraton hotel known as the Miramar is a five-star resort consisting of over 400 guestrooms and public spaces such as food and beverage facilities. Dramatically sited on the Red Sea, the project is bounded on all sides by water or shoreline. The landscaped grounds feature a myriad of canals and lagoons, providing each guestroom with a waterfront orientation. The elaborate swimming pool complex includes picturesque adult pools, an exercise pool and a pool for children. Built using traditional Egyptian vernacular construction methods and materials, the guestrooms feature brick vaulted and domed ceilings. The great variety in the forms and detailing of the hotel creates a unique resort that reflects its desert and waterfront context in an elegant and often surprising manner.

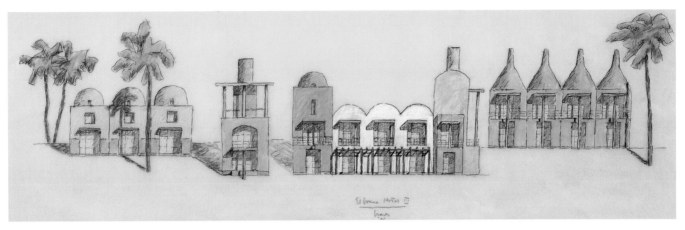

*Character study*

*Main building entrance elevation*

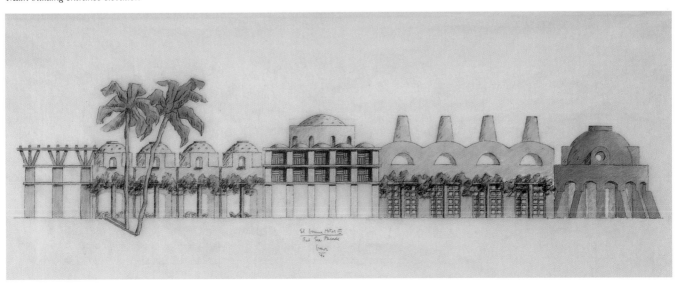

*Main building beachfront elevation*

59

View from the beach

*Guestroom pavilions detail*

*Guestroom pavilions detail*

Suite sitting room

Typical guestroom

# Riverfront Sports Complex Master Plan

*Cincinnati, Ohio, 1995*

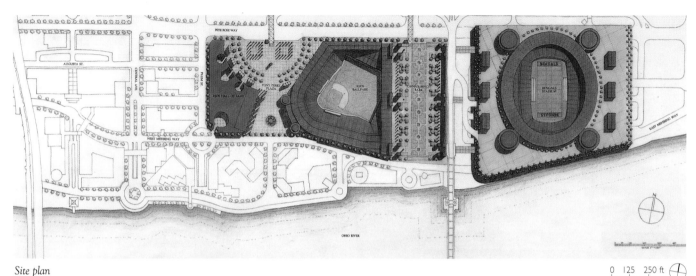

*Site plan*

0  125  250 ft

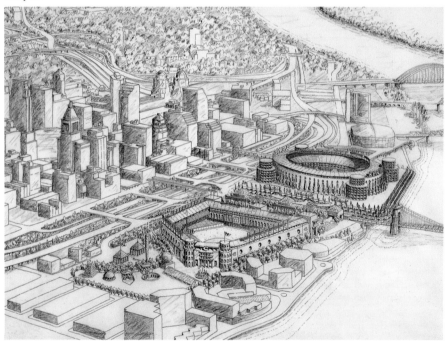

*Aerial view from the Ohio River*

The master plan for the Riverfront Sports Complex in Cincinnati was prepared to assist Hamilton County in its successful campaign to obtain public funding for the development. The master plan provides independent sports facilities for baseball and football, integrated into a complex of public places such as a park, a plaza and entertainment centers. The proposal to clad the buildings in brick is intended to reinforce continuity with the character of the urban surroundings.

The 45,000-seat ballpark for the Cincinnati Reds baseball team is sited so that it does not interfere with either the city fabric or views toward the Ohio River from neighboring streets. A public plaza adjacent to the ballpark also accommodates entertainment activities, restaurants, retail shops and a hall of fame. The master plan recommended replacement of the outmoded Riverfront Stadium with a new football stadium configured around the needs, traditions and rules of the game.

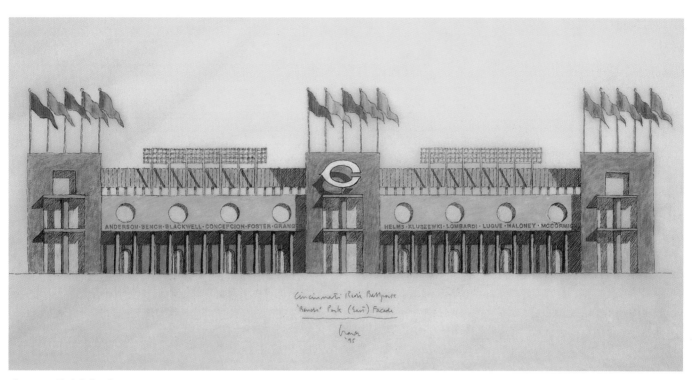

*Cincinnati Reds ballpark*

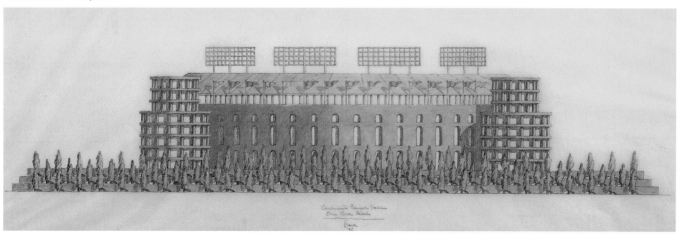

*Cincinnati Bengals football stadium*

# Laurel Hall
# New Jersey Institute of Technology

*Newark, New Jersey, 1995 and 2000*

In conjunction with a master plan prepared by Michael Graves & Associates
for the New Jersey Institute of
Technology, a series of projects establish a residential quadrangle for undergraduate students at the southeast edge
of the urban campus. Laurel Hall, a
300-bed student residence that was the
first project to be built, forms the lon-
gitudinal boundary of a new campus
green opposite the school's parking
deck. Oak Hall, a former industrial
building previously converted to student housing, establishes the far
boundary of the green. A new color
scheme for Oak Hall's facades was created to complement Laurel Hall.
These projects were followed several
years later by an expansion of Laurel
Hall, which approximately doubled
its capacity. The expansion, extending
along Warren Street perpendicular to
the original building, completes the
fourth side of the open space.

Laurel Hall's centralized entrance
portico, with four-story aluminum
columns supporting a thin flat roof,
acts as a symbolic front porch. In order
to lend a residential scale to the
lengthy facades of the building, the
single rooms and stairs are recessed
from the plane of the facades and
finished with dark gray-blue stucco
as if in deep shadow.

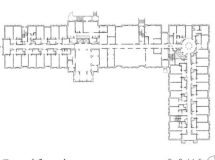

*Ground floor plan*                 0  8  16 ft

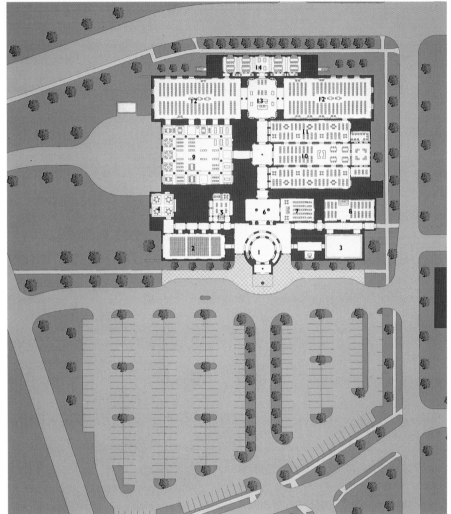

1 Rotunda foyer
2 Multipurpose room
3 Gallery
4 Café
5 Bookstore
6 Circulation desk
7 Red Carpet services
8 Audio-visual collection
9 Reference/Periodicals
10 Children's library
11 Young Adult Collection
12 Adult Collection
13 Service desk
14 Reading room

*Site and ground floor plan*

0  25  50 ft

# Main Library of Topeka and Shawnee County

*Topeka, Kansas, 1995*

Upon the 125th anniversary of its founding, the Main Library of Topeka and Shawnee County commissioned the renovation of its 65,000-square-foot facility built in the 1950s and an expansion of 100,000 square feet. The expansion wraps around the existing structure, resulting in redesigned facades that establish a new identity for this important public institution.

A three-story rotunda on axis with Washburn Street creates a new public entrance facing adjacent parking. Flanking the entrance are several community facilities, including a 360-seat auditorium, a café, a bookstore and a 3,500-square-foot art gallery. The circular lobby reinforces the communality of these amenities and leads to the Topeka Room on the third level. Large circular skylights allow natural light to enter the building during the day and create a monumental beacon when lit from within at night. Internally, the intersection of the building's east-west and north-south axes is distinguished by an atrium lit from above by a skylight. The atrium allows users to orient themselves within the library and gain access to the surrounding Adult Collections, Periodicals and Youth Services Departments.

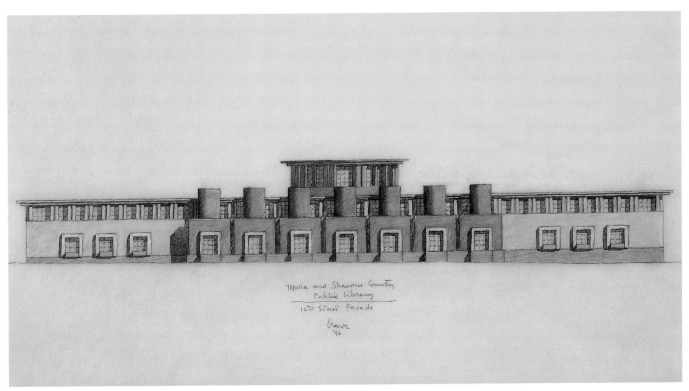

Preliminary 10th Street elevation

Model view from the south showing main entrance

*Facing page top: Entrance*
*Facing page bottom: Reading room facade detail*

Reading room

Atrium

O'Reilly Theater

*Pittsburgh, Pennsylvania, 1996*

Service center from Penn Avenue

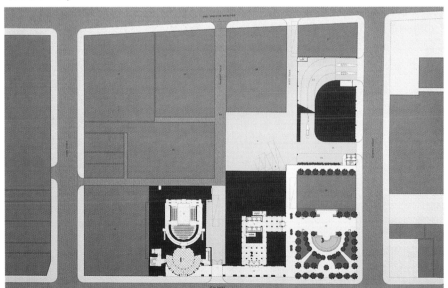

Site and ground floor plan

1 O'Reilly Theater
2 Service center
3 Park

0   30   60 ft

*Lobby view from second floor.*

The O'Reilly is a 650-seat legitimate theater located on Penn Avenue in Pittsburgh's Cultural District. The massing and composition of the building continue the existing streetwall while establishing a distinctive identity appropriate to a cultural institution. A curved overhanging copper roof and backlit building sign define the entrance and double-height lobby. The circular forms in plan and section foreshadow the shape of the auditorium and help define a unified experience for the theater audience.

The auditorium has a thrust stage around which the audience is seated on three levels, providing an intimate venue for repertory theater and chamber music. The differing acoustic needs of these two performance types were met through the shape of the space, the articulation of the surfaces and the choice of construction materials.

The project included the design of a public park in conjunction with landscape architect Dan Kiley and sculptor Louise Bourgeois. An adjacent service center, constructed in a subsequent phase, contains eight levels of parking above a ground floor with retail shops, a cabaret theater and a ticket office serving various venues within the Cultural District.

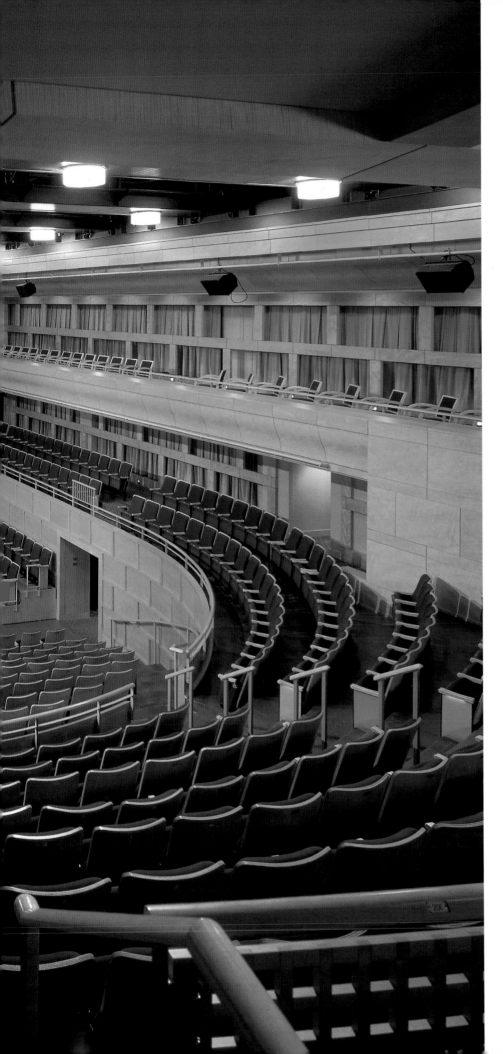

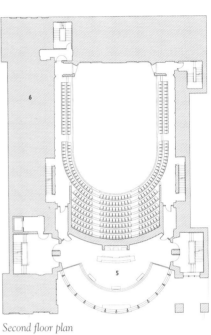

*Second floor plan*

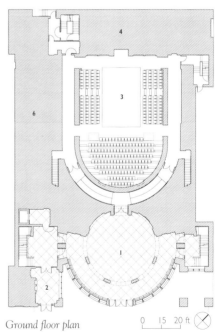

*Ground floor plan*

0   15   20 ft

1 Lobby
2 Tickets
3 Theater
4 Backstage
5 Intermission bar
6 Offices

*Second floor intermission bar*

*Mural cartoon*

**Hyatt Regency Hotel**
*Taba Heights, Egypt, 1996*

*Guestroom groups facing the lagoon*

*Site plan*

0  20  40 m

The Hyatt Regency Hotel in Taba Heights is a five-star resort with 426 guestrooms, situated on the mountainous Sinai Peninsula facing the Bay of Aqaba. The main building, with its strong axial entrance and palm court, embraces a large terrace, where a restaurant, bar and other activities look out over manmade rock formations toward the sea. The outlying guestroom groups are sited in the hilly terrain so as to preserve views of the water from all quarters.

As with its companion project, the Sheraton Miramar Resort Hotel in El Gouna, which was designed for the same developer, the architecture is distinguished by the variety of building shapes and details. The character of the buildings, through massing, materials and facades, as well as through the custom-designed interior furnishings,

relates in an abstract way to the traditions of rural Egyptian architecture. Built using typical Egyptian construction methods and materials, many of the guestrooms feature brick vaulted or domed ceilings.

*Pool snack bar*

Pool court

View toward the Gulf of Aqaba

Stair tower

Facing page: Restaurant

Bar

*Guestroom*

# World Trade Exchange Center

*Manila, Philippines, 1996*

The World Trade Exchange Center is a mixed-use building 35 stories high, located in Metro Manila's historic district near Manila Bay and the Pasig River. The massing, fenestration patterns and coloration articulate the various uses of the building. The base contains two floors of retail space. Above it are six floors of parking with openings in the facade shielded by awninglike metal louvers. The upper portion of the building, used principally for offices, is divided horizontally in two sections to help diminish the scale of the building in deference to its midrise neighbors. The cylindrical corner tower features expansive windows facing Manila Bay.

*Calle Nimfa elevation*

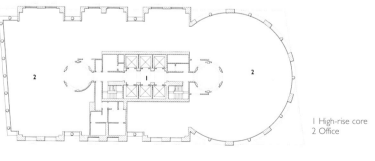

1 High-rise core
2 Office

*Typical office floor plan*

0    5    10 m

# Ortigas Tycoon Twin Towers

*Ortigas, Philippines, 1996*

The Ortigas Tycoon Twin Towers is a mixed-use development consisting of two 38-story towers rising above a six-story plinth. The plinth contains retail and recreational facilities on the lowest levels and a parking garage above, characterized by awninglike metal louvers along the long horizontal facades. One of the towers contains office space and the other a condominium hotel.

*Southeast elevation*

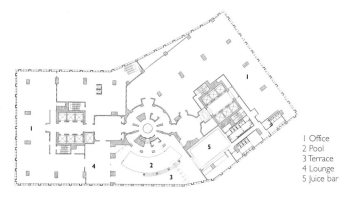

1 Office
2 Pool
3 Terrace
4 Lounge
5 Juice bar

*Plinth plan at health club level*

0 5 10 m

**Miele Americas Headquarters**

*Princeton, New Jersey, 1996 and 1999*

*Lobby*

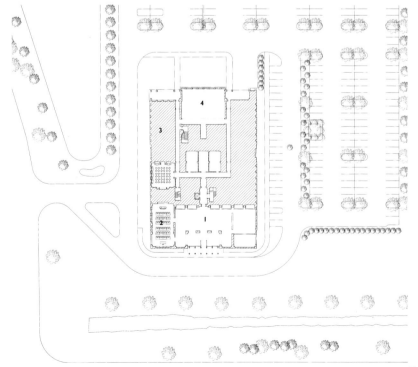

The Americas headquarters of this international company specializing in high-quality household appliances is located on Route One near Princeton. Its brightly lit entrance pavilion topped by a large-scale sign allows the building to be easily identified from the highway.

The ground floor accommodates a large showroom to welcome visitors and provide display areas for various Miele products. A double-height portion of the showroom is enclosed in glass, allowing the space to be flooded with natural light during the day and become a glowing landmark at night. Surrounding the showroom are various spaces for the presentation of Miele products, including demonstration stations, a large training room and meeting rooms. The second floor is used for Miele's offices.

A planned expansion that doubled the size of the building was implemented soon after the completion of the first phase.

1 Showroom
2 Demonstration kitchen
3 Meeting room
4 Technical support

*Site and ground floor plan*

0  16  32 ft

# Fujian Xingye Bank

*Shanghai, China, 1996*

The Fujian Xingye Bank, upon acquiring a site in the historic district of Shanghai near the Courthouse and Customs Building and facing the Bund, commissioned alternative conceptual designs for a 26-story mixed-use building. The lower 10 floors would contain banking facilities as well as retail and office space. The tower would contain tenant office space. These several functions of the building are expressed through massing, architectural design, materials and colors. The bank subsequently sold the site and the project designed by Michael Graves & Associates did not proceed.

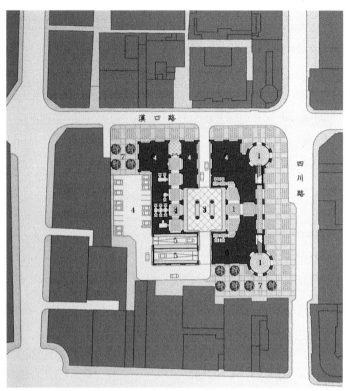

*Site and ground floor plan*

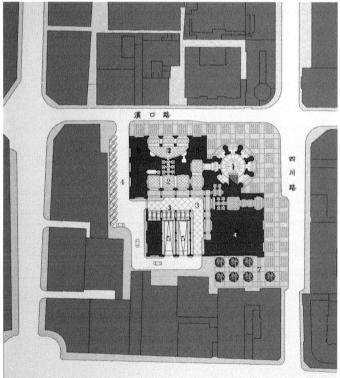

*Preliminary site and ground floor plan*

1 Bank lobby
2 Office tower lobby
3 Motor court
4 Retail

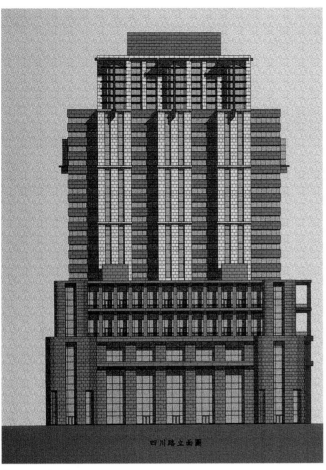

四川路立面圖

Entrance elevation

漢口路立面圖

Side elevation

四川路立面圖

Preliminary entrance elevation

漢口路立面圖

Preliminary side elevation

# Lake Hills Country Club

*Seoul, Korea, 1996*

*Lobby*

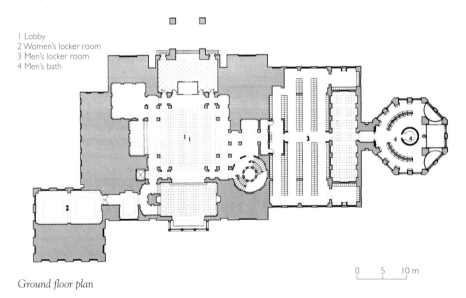

1 Lobby
2 Women's locker room
3 Men's locker room
4 Men's bath

0  5  10 m

*Ground floor plan*

*Facing page: Golf course facade*

The clubhouse for Lake Hills Country Club in Seoul overlooks the golf course and contains a restaurant, breakfast room, baths and changing rooms for men and women, as well as golf cart storage and other service spaces. The men's baths are located in the octagonal tower, and the women's baths are located in a pavilion at the opposite end of the building.

As a building type, a golf club embodies the spirit of sport, camaraderie and the pleasures of domestic comfort. At the client's request, the clubhouse was given an architectural character intended to recall a traditional manor house, an inviting and familiar place for members and their guests.

# Library of the French Institute/Alliance Française

*New York, New York, 1996*

The French Institute/Alliance Française is located in a historic townhouse at 22 East 60th Street in the Upper East Side of Manhattan. Its library is housed in approximately 5,800 square feet on the second and third floors. In this complete renovation of the library, the second floor accommodates public spaces, including the reception room and gallery, the main reading room, the reference room, a computer learning center and the children's collection. Openings in the ceiling provide visual connection to the stacks located on the third floor.

*Reading room*

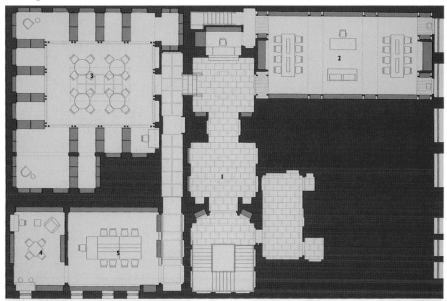

*Second floor plan*

1 Reception
2 Reference/Periodicals
3 Reading room
4 Children's collection
5 Computer workstations

0    8    16 ft

*East 60th Street elevation*

## LIFE Magazine
## Dream House

*1996*

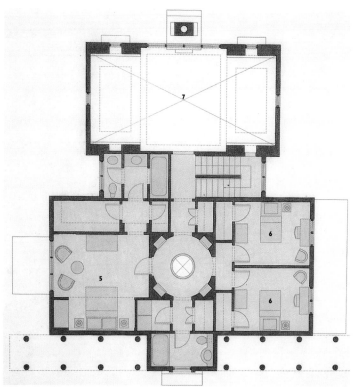

1 Foyer
2 Kitchen
3 Garage
4 Living/dining room
5 Master bedroom
6 Bedroom
7 Open to below

*Second floor plan*

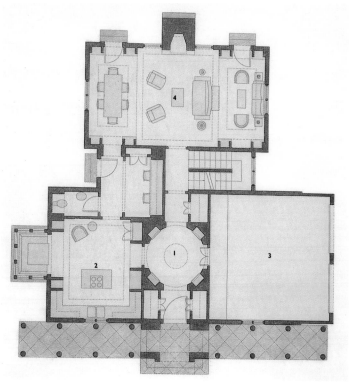

*Ground floor plan*

0    8    16 ft

LIFE Magazine commissioned Michael Graves to design its third annual prototypical "Dream House." LIFE's goal was to show its readers that a well-known architect could create a house design comparable in size and cost to the average new house being built in the United States. The design anticipates flexibility in its plans and materials in order to be adaptable to the requirements of various families and sites.

The rotunda foyer is central to the organization of the plan and sets up the procession through the house. The orderly nature of the architecture and interiors allows the owners to achieve a comfortable sense of well-being in the house and to personalize it for their lifestyles.

*LIFE Magazine cover*

*Street elevation*

*Kitchen*

*Living/dining room*

House at Indian Hill

*Cincinnati, Ohio, 1996*

*View toward house from studio and potting shed*

*Potting shed*

Located on a 3.5-acre lot adjacent to heavily wooded public parkland, and overlooking the Little Miami River, this 6,000-square-foot house uses an L-shaped configuration to engage the surrounding landscape. The massing consists of 10 distinct pavilions carefully arranged within a building area constrained by zoning requirements. The pavilions evolved from different programmatic uses and are individualized through distinctive shapes, colors and materials.

A formal tripartite facade and a square paved forecourt mark the entry to the house. Views to the river are framed in a variety of ways from the vaulted living room, the study, the dining room, the solarium and the master bedroom's elevated covered terrace. A guest wing above the three-car garage is connected to the main house by a circular stair tower clad with fieldstone. A path from the sheltered court at the rear of the house leads past a pyramidal pool house and swimming pool and into the parkland beyond. At the far end of the site, set in a field near the river, a folly affectionately called the "potting shed" contains a greenhouse and a small studio.

*Facing page: Living room*

*View from the east*

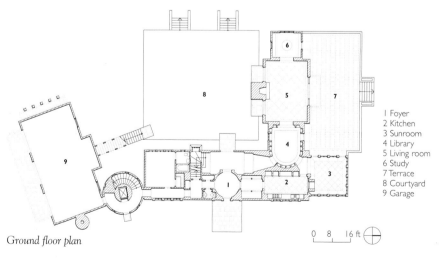

*Ground floor plan*

1 Foyer
2 Kitchen
3 Sunroom
4 Library
5 Living room
6 Study
7 Terrace
8 Courtyard
9 Garage

0   8   16 ft

*Dining room*

# Kolonihaven House

*Copenhagen, Denmark, 1996*

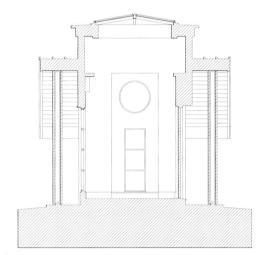

*Section*

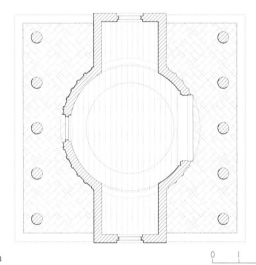

*Plan*

0 | 2 m

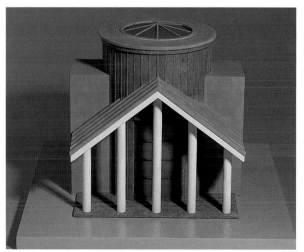

*Model view of the entrance*

To celebrate Copenhagen as the 1996 European Cultural Capital, 14 internationally known architects were commissioned to reinterpret the "Kolonihaven House," a traditional building type found in Danish garden colonies. These small structures of approximately 7.5 square meters range from simple farm buildings to colorfully decorated pleasure pavilions found in romantic gardens. In their simplest form, they invoke the pleasures of summer gardening to provide sustenance for the household as well as an idyllic escape from the hectic nature of urban life. Michael Graves & Associates' version of the Kolonihaven House consists of a simple rotunda flanked by porches that connect the house to the garden.

In addition to being exhibited through drawings and models, the Kolonihaven Houses are to be constructed in Denmark's first architecture park in Vallenbæk, south of Copenhagen.

*Entrance elevation*

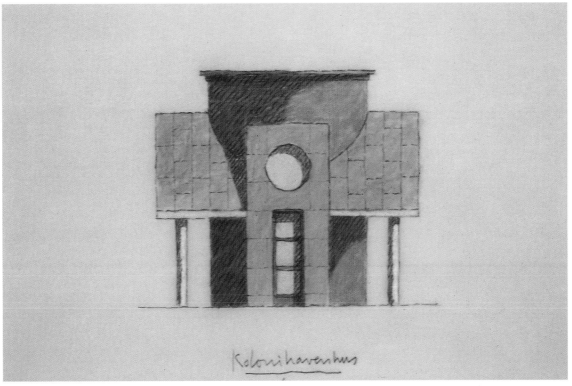

*Side elevation*

# Charles E. Beatley, Jr. Central Library

*Alexandria, Virginia, 1996*

*Entrance elevation*

The several programmatic functions of the 45,000-square-foot Charles E. Beatley, Jr. Central Library are composed as distinctive volumes around a semi-public courtyard, creating a massing strategy reminiscent of a village square. The library has two primary facades, one forming the entrance from Pickett Street, and the other providing a public presence along Duke Street. The building is topped by a dozen roofs that recall the community's roots in Old Town. The resulting silhouette symbolizes the first step toward the city's master plan goal of establishing a new civic center on the west side of Alexandria.

The interior of the library is open in plan. However, the various departments are distinguished by the configuration of the ceilings, which reflect the distinctive roof structures.

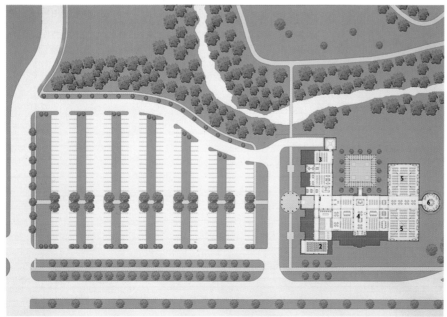

*Site and ground floor plan*

1 Lobby
2 Community room
3 Children's library
4 Reference
5 Adult collection
6 Periodicals

0    50    100 ft

*Facing page: Reading room*

View from Duke Street

East facade

FRANK AND BETTY WRIGHT
READING GARDEN
A GIFT OF THE FRANK AND BETTY WRIGHT FOUNDATION

# Uffelman Country House

*Reading, Connecticut, 1997*

*Garden elevation*

At the client's request, this weekend house draws its inspiration from the tradition of decorative pavilions or follies found in romantic country gardens. As amusements that provide escape from the realities of everyday life, such buildings are often playful and picturesque.

This country house is sited at the top of a hill from where it overlooks a private golf, rolling wooded terrain and a pond. The four-story fieldstone stair tower in the center of the house leads to a study on the top floor. The tower is flanked by two multistory wings that are given the character of festive striped tents. One wing contains the living room and guest bedroom, and the other contains a family room, dining room, kitchen and bedrooms.

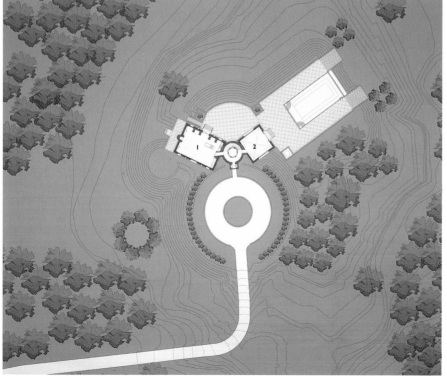

*Site and ground floor plan*

0    25    50 ft

1 Kitchen and
  dining/family room
2 Living room

*Stair hall from above*

*Living room*

# Rearrangement of the Florence Cathedral Choir

*Florence, Italy, 1997*

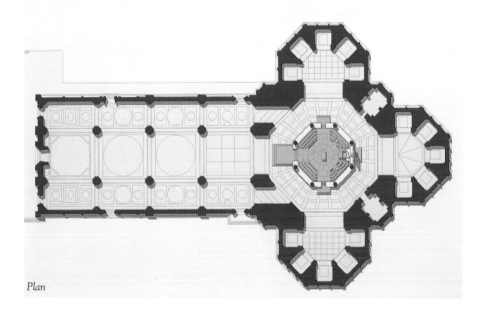

*Sectional model showing baldachin*

*Plan*

Several architects were invited to participate in an "international consultation" concerning the rearrangement of the choir of the Florence Cathedral. The choir, located beneath the magnificent Renaissance dome by Filippo Brunelleschi, culminates the nave and marks the crossing with an octagonal walled enclosure within which mass is celebrated. To contemporary ecclesiastic sensibilities, the choir enclosure is a barrier, separating clergy from the assembly area and limiting participation of the faithful in church rituals. Rearrangement of altar, pulpit, seating and the sculpture by Baccio Bandinelli were to meet current liturgical needs while respecting the original concept.

The proposal to center a new framelike baldachin beneath the dome takes into account centroidal and linear readings of the architecture. The form of the baldachin relates to the dome above, and its wooden structure is more open and ephemeral in comparison to the surrounding church. The platform below the baldachin is raised above floor level to resolve the current lack of visibility. From the platform, an apron extends toward the nave, acknowledging the linear progression of the basilican church plan and providing a functional setting for celebratory rituals.

*Sketch of Bandinelli sculpture*

*Photo collage of baldachin in the cathedral*

NCAA Headquarters and
Hall of Champions

*Indianapolis, Indiana, 1997*

*Commemorative print by Michael Graves*

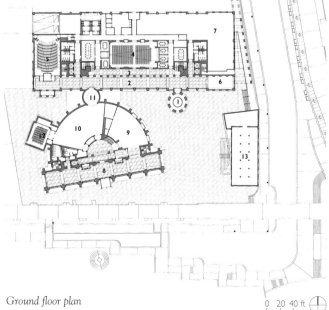

*Ground floor plan*

0  20  40 ft

1 Office building entrance
2 Atrium
3 Prefunction
4 Multipurpose room
5 Auditorium
6 Boardroom
7 Library
8 Hall of Champions
  Great Hall
9 Gift shop
10 Exhibit
11 Champions room
12 Auditorium
13 High school federation
   offices

The headquarters office building, conference center, and Hall of Champions of the National Collegiate Athletic Association occupies a prominent site on the Central Canal in White River State Park in Indianapolis. The complex is composed as a series of interconnected structures that create a campuslike setting, which both reflects the character of the park and refers to the collegiate atmosphere of the NCAA's member institutions.

The 140,000-square-foot program for the offices and conference center is accommodated in a four-story block at the north side of the site. Upper floor offices look over a full-height internal atrium and the entrance plaza. The simple massing of the office building allows it to serve as a backdrop for the more specialized features of the project: the Hall of Champions and the historic Acme Evans Superintendent's Building, which houses a high school athletic organization.

The 40,000-square-foot program for the Hall of Champions includes a 90-seat theater and two floors of exhibitions featuring the history of the NCAA and the achievements of teams and individual scholar-athletes. It is entered through an arcade reminiscent of collegiate athletic facilities in which a 45-foot-high lobby gallery is open to the public without charge.

*Hall of Champions*

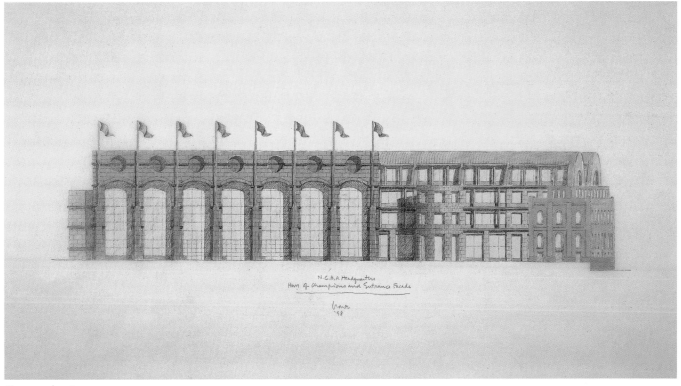

*Entrance elevation*

*Upper floor offices*

# Fortis AG Headquarters

*Brussels, Belgium, 1997*

*Lobby*

The headquarters office building for the Belgian banking, insurance and real estate company Fortis AG is located at No. 53 Boulevard Emile Jacqmain in the heart of the historic old pentagon of Brussels. There was an existing building on the site that was extensively reworked inside and given new facades as part of this project. Michael Graves & Associates, working with two local architects, was responsible for the design of the facades and public lobby. In response to the traditional nature of the context, the exterior is reminiscent of characteristically Belgian facade rhythms, materials and detailing but at the same time presents a fresh and contemporary public image for the company.

El Gouna Golf Hotel and Club

*El Gouna, Egypt, 1997*

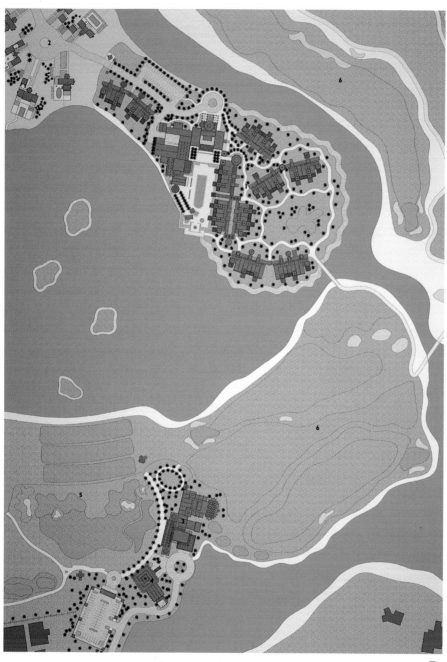

The El Gouna Golf Hotel and Club are the centerpieces of a golf and villa development on the Red Sea at the end of a large peninsula among the lagoons of the 18-hole El Gouna golf course.

The Golf Hotel contains 208 guestrooms and serviced apartments. The main building steps down towards a long lap pool with wide terraces orienting views over the lagoon to the golf clubhouse and pyramid-shaped restaurant. Clusters of guestroom groups are built around the edge of the peninsula, with the terraces of individual units overlooking the surrounding golf course. Large putting greens and golf cart parking bring golfers to the public areas of the hotel. A bar and game room is located on the upper level with views over the roofs of the guestrooms.

The clubhouse contains a pro shop, golf pro offices, lockers, a health club with Turkish baths and a long viewing terrace that overlooks the practice green and the golf course. A separate restaurant and bar take the form of a tall truncated pyramid atop a viewing platform. The entire golf course and the sea beyond can be seen from this pyramid.

1 Golf hotel
2 Golf villas
3 Golf club
4 Restaurant
5 Golf practice area
6 Golf course

*Site plan*

0   20   40 m

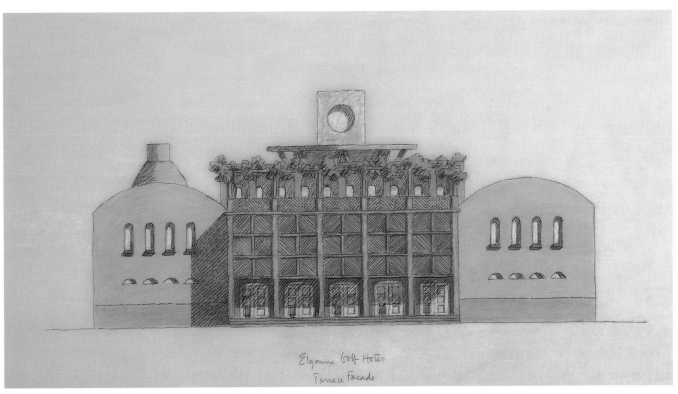

*Main building entrance elevation*

*Main building terrace elevation*

137

Pool court

Pool court

*Left: Health club pools*

*Café terrace*

*Right: Lobby*

*Following pages: View of golf clubhouse
and restaurant pavilion*

Guestroom

Golf Villas

*El Gouna, Egypt, 1997*

*Villa, construction photograph*

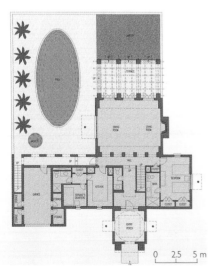

*Villa type 1, ground floor plan*

*Villa type 4, ground floor plan*

The golf villas, a golf hotel and a clubhouse comprise an extensive development sited on a large peninsula surrounded by seawater lagoons and oriented toward the 18-hole golf course in El Gouna. The character of the villas is related to the architecture of the nearby golf hotel and clubhouse, which recall traditional Egyptian rural architecture.

The villas are intended as casual vacation and weekend retreats. The organization of their living areas around an outdoor terrace, swimming pool and garden establishes an easy flow between indoors and outdoors. Six distinct villa designs were prepared, ranging in size from 200 to 300 square meters and including options for adding garages, servants quarters and more bedrooms.

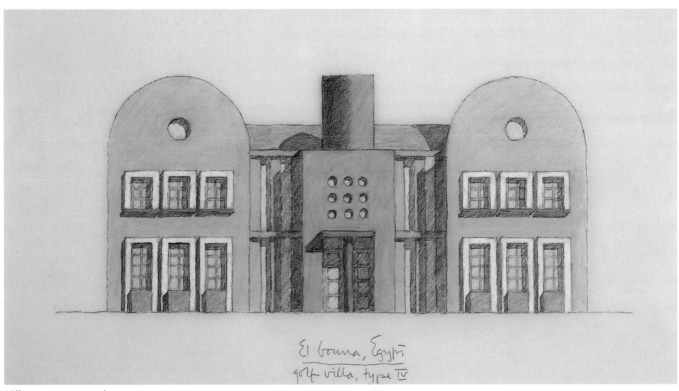

*Villa type 1, entrance elevation*

*Villa type 4, entrance elevation*

# De Luwte

*On the River Vecht, Netherlands, 1997*

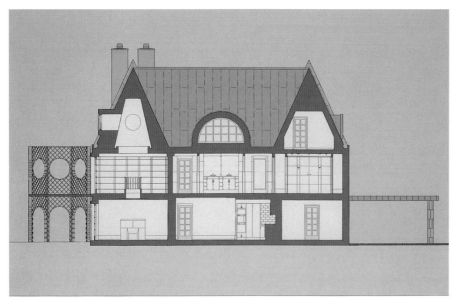

*Section*

De Luwte is a single-family house located on the banks of the River Vecht near Amsterdam. In order to emphasize the importance of the relationship between the house and the river, the client named the house De Luwte, which translates as "The Lee," a shelter from wind and water. The living room, master bedroom and study look out to the water, while the kitchen and dining room open onto riverfront terraces. The outdoor spaces are designed as extensions of the interiors so that there is an easy transition between the house and the outdoors. The semicircular stair provides a graceful means of moving between floors and draws light into the center of the house.

The Dutch tradition of gabled roofs and brick construction is reinterpreted in the massing and materials used in the house.

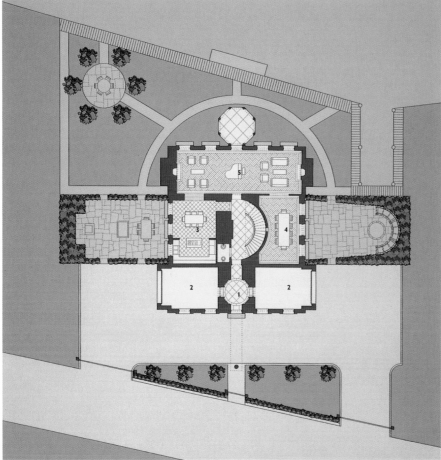

1 Foyer
2 Garage
3 Kitchen
4 Dining room
5 Living room

*Site and ground floor plan*

0   4   8 m

*Garden elevation study*

*Entrance elevation study*

151

# InterContinental Hotel

*Taba Heights, Egypt, 1997*

*Construction photographs of guestroom group*

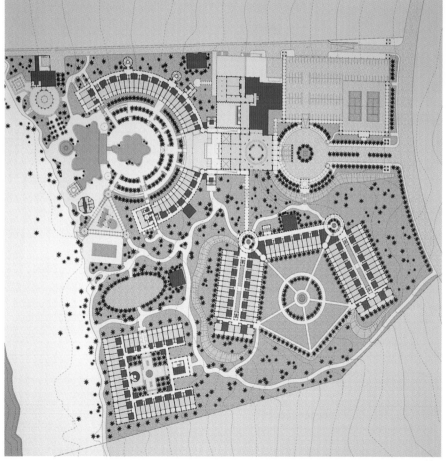

The InterContinental beach resort hotel located on the Aqaba Bay is a 500-room, international five-star hotel. The three-story main building is entered on the upper floor and, following the rather steep slope of the land, steps down to the restaurant and the health club levels. The guestrooms are organized in three large clusters, each with its own shape and character. Throughout the resort, there are surprising views to the bay, with a foreground of lively beach restaurants and bars surrounding generous swimming pools.

*Site and ground floor plan*

0    25    50 m

*Courtyard elevation of guestroom group*

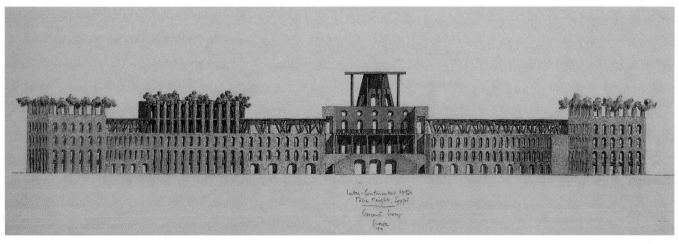

*Courtyard elevation of guestroom group*

153

*45th Street elevation*

# Competition for Hotel Sofitel

*New York, New York, 1997*

Hotel Sofitel occupies a through-block site between West 44th and 45th Street Streets near Fifth Avenue in New York City. The site measures the width of a typical brownstone on West 44th Street, where the developer wanted the entrance to be located, and widens to approximately 100 feet on West 45th Street. The entrance pavilion, with a marquee featuring a new logotype for the hotel, is four stories tall and conforms to the prevailing context. The midblock contains a thin tower with additional projecting logotypes, connected to the main body of the hotel facing 45th Street. This scheme was not selected for further development.

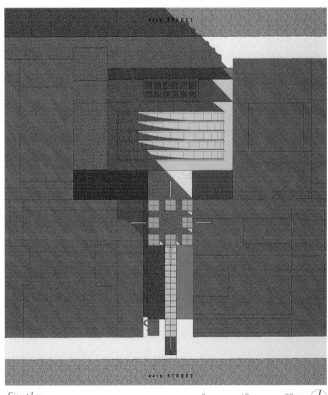

*Site plan*

*Model view from 45th Street*

# North Hall
# Drexel University

*Philadelphia, Pennsylvania, 1997*

*View from the southeast*

North Hall is a 171,300-square-foot student residence that occupies an entire city block between Race and Cherry Streets at the edge of the Drexel University campus adjacent to the Powellton Village residential neighborhood. The building is organized in two six-story wings connected at each floor by a circular stair tower that serves as the main public space. The residence hall accommodates 500 students in a combination of four- and six-person apartment-style suites.

The building is urban in character, but rather than establishing a streetwall along the property line, the design reserves the corner of the site at Cherry and 33rd Streets as open green space, creating a transition from the city to the adjacent neighborhood. The organization of the building in two wings helps to break down the scale in deference to the residential scale of the neighborhood. The top floor of each wing is expressed as an attic story reminiscent of traditional Philadelphia-area architecture.

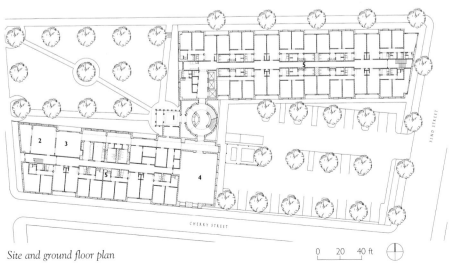

*Site and ground floor plan*

1 Entrance
2 Game room
3 Lounge
4 Meeting room
5 Suites

0   20   40 ft

*South facade detail*

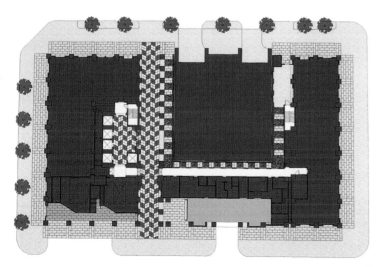

*Facade detail*

# Mixed-use Building

*Fukuoka, Japan, 1997*

This 10-story, 24,000-square-meter speculative development is located near Hakata Station in the most prominent office district in Fukuoka. The program includes retail shops at the base of the building and high-quality rental offices above. The U-shaped site wraps around an existing structure in the middle of the block. The composition of the new building creates pavilion-like projections on the building's facades, which create a continuous context surrounding the existing building.

*Site and ground floor plan*

0  5  10 m

## United States Courthouse
### *Washington, D.C., 1997*

*Courtroom*

This project for the United States Federal District Courts involves renovation of the existing 576,500-square-foot Prettyman Courthouse and new construction of a 351,000-square-foot Annex. The Annex contains courtsets for the U.S. District and Appellate Courts, chambersets for the District and the Court of Appeals and offices. The program also includes extensive ancillary functions such as a food service complex, library, health unit, press room, fitness center, credit union and other support facilities.

Located at Constitution and Pennsylvania Avenues and within sight of the Capitol, the Annex defines a pivotal point in the city. Its massing and organization respond to contextual challenges while addressing the institutional values and practical requirements of a courthouse. Critical to the contextual response is the rotunda at the intersection of Pennsylvania and Constitution Avenues. Internally, a key feature of the Annex is the atrium, which links the existing and new structures and introduces natural light into adjacent interiors, particularly the courtrooms in the Annex.

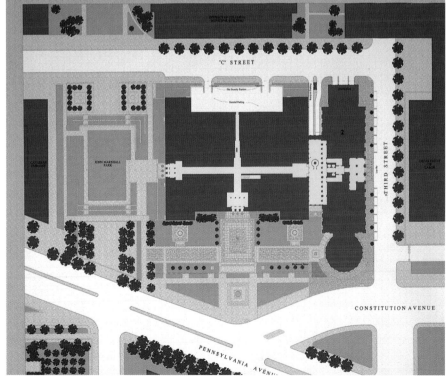

*Site and ground floor plan*

1 Existing courthouse
2 Annex

0 8 16 m

*Third Street elevation*

*View from Pennsylvania and Constitution Avenues*

# Ogoori Plaza

*Ogoori, Japan, 1997*

A feasibility study for an extensive new development encompassed the renovation of the Ogoori Railroad Station and construction of an extensive mixed-use complex on a site to the north of the station. Among the functions planned for the development are a business hotel, a tour bus depot, a department store and other retail shops, a cultural hall accommodating approximately 3000 people, a multiplex cinema, residences and parking.

*Train station and bus depot elevation*

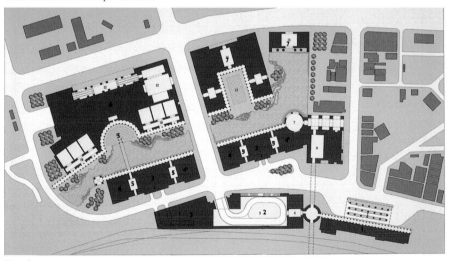

*Site plan*

1 Ogoori Railroad Station
2 Bus depot
3 Parking
4 Retail/restaurant, residential above
5 Riverwalk plaza
6 Cultural hall
7 Office building

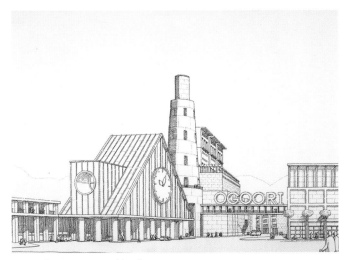

View of train station and hotel

View along Riverwalk

# Hotel Makati

*Manila, Philippines, 1997*

Hotel Makati is a 27-story mixed-use development located between Kalayaan Avenue and Alfonso Street in Manila. It contains approximately 26,000 square meters of commercial, parking, recreational, hotel and residential uses. There are 300 rooms for hotel and service apartments.

*Site and ground floor plan*

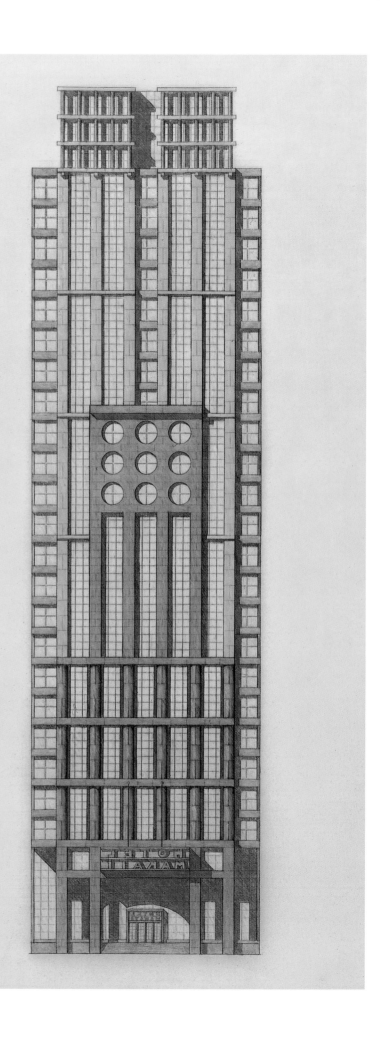

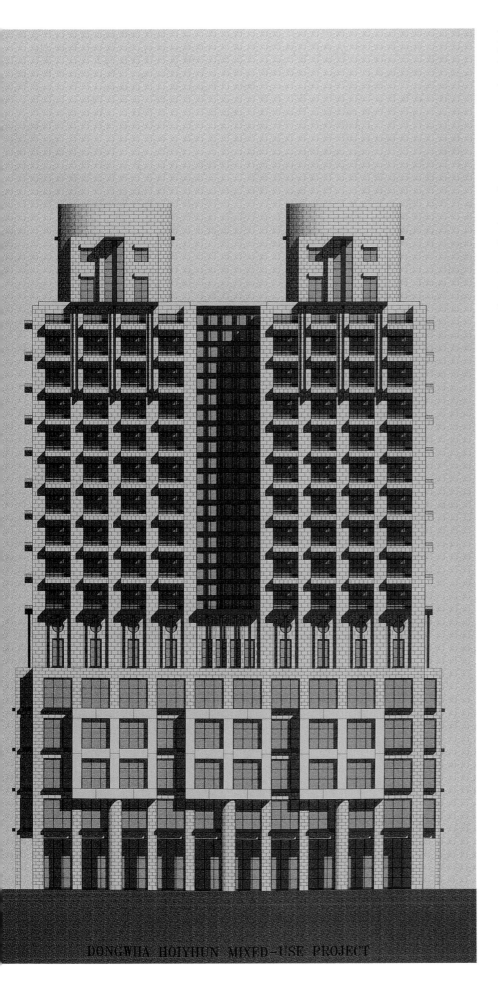

# Dongwha Hoiyun Mixed-use Building

*Seoul, Korea, 1997*

The proposed mixed-use building located in the Hoiyhun Redevelopment Area in Seoul has 33 floors above grade and eight below. Included in the approximately 137,500-square-meter program are residential apartments, commercial offices, a discount department store, athletic facilities, and parking.

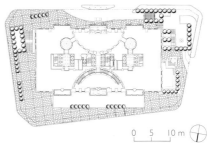

0   5   10 m

*Site and ground floor plan*

DONGWHA HOIYHUN MIXED-USE PROJECT

# O'Grady Library
## Saint Martin's College

*Lacey, Washington, 1997*

Saint Martin's College is a Benedictine institution that serves students living on campus as well as commuting from the surrounding area. The O'Grady Library, which houses collections of books and other media and provides instructional space, is central to the college's educational program and the students' academic pursuits while on campus. The site, located in a developing area of the campus, slopes steeply down from existing academic buildings toward the entrance road and thus offers the possibility of establishing a new, visible academic core distinct from the more private monastic zone of the other side of campus.

The building is organized around a central core of stacks and collection areas, lit from above by clerestory windows. Reading and study areas around the perimeter of the building provide natural light and views of the surrounding forest. The building's character relates to Saint Martin's Benedictine traditions and adjacent campus buildings through the use of pointed arch windows and other familiar detailing.

*Entrance facade*

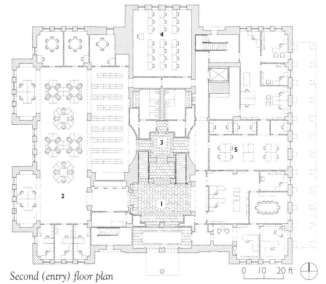

*Second (entry) floor plan*

1 Lobby
2 Reference
3 Stair hall
4 Computer
5 Media services

0   10   20 ft

*Circulation desk*

*View along East 76th Street*

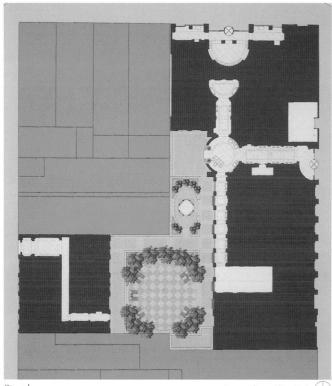

*Site plan*

0    12    24 ft

# The Impala

*New York, New York, 1997*

This 268,000-square-foot rental apartment and condominium complex contains approximately 200 residential units in three buildings around a landscaped courtyard. Design challenges included the necessity of working within a narrow range of massing options dictated by zoning. Facing First Avenue, the building contains commercial and retail spaces. Medical offices are located on 76th Street side. Most of the housing is located in a 24-story tower above a seven-story base. The Impala's residential lobby faces the building's private courtyard garden, while the massing maintains the street edge that typifies local residential neighborhoods.

Aesthetically, the design takes as a starting point some of the traditional residential buildings of New York City, particularly those on the Upper East Side. The articulation surrounding the windows is expanded in scale to modulate the size of the apartment tower as a whole. Thus, two stories read as one through the double-height precast frames around the windows. The combination of red brick and white trim is reminiscent of materials and colors associated with neo-Georgian residential architecture, although expressed at the scale of the urban context.

*Facing page: Courtyard*

*Lobby looking toward reception desk*

*Model apartment living room*

## Study for a Private Residence

*Long Island, New York, 1997*

This residence for a family of six is designed like a rambling English manor house in which individually articulated pavilions house different internal functions. This strategy preserves a domestic scale while accommodating an expansive program, and allows the house to engage the surrounding landscape. The long drive into the site through an existing allée of trees terminates in a circular courtyard and a crescent-shaped library. The house is entered at the lower level, but the primary living spaces are located on the *piano nobile*. The crescent balances the living room on one side with the master bedroom suite on the other. A separate children's wing contains bedrooms on the upper level and a playroom and media room below.

*Preliminary elevation with entrance courtyard in foreground*

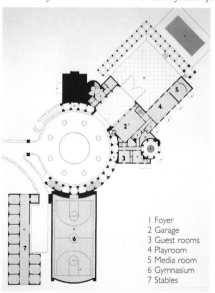

1 Foyer
2 Garage
3 Guest rooms
4 Playroom
5 Media room
6 Gymnasium
7 Stables

*Preliminary ground floor plan*

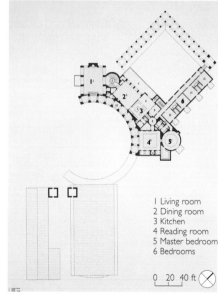

1 Living room
2 Dining room
3 Kitchen
4 Reading room
5 Master bedroom
6 Bedrooms

0  20  40 ft

*Preliminary second floor plan*

*Model view of the entrance and courtyard*

The Washington Monument
Restoration

*Washington, D.C., 1998*

*Scaffolding detail*

When the Washington Monument needed major restoration work to combat years of weathering and aging, a public-private partnership of the National Park Service and Target Stores commissioned the design of the scaffolding, which surrounded the monument for three years, as well as the redesign of the interior observation and interpretive areas. The scaffolding, which was engineered by the contractor, followed the profile of the monument. It was embellished with a blue semi-transparent architectural mesh fabric attached in a running bond masonry pattern that reflected the monument's stone mortar joints at a larger scale. At night, the scaffolding was lit from within by hundreds of lights.

By allowing a view of the restoration work being performed behind the scaffolding, the design appropriately allowed visitors to gain an appreciation for the importance of the task. In a sense, two monuments were presented to the public: the one being restored, and the one erected for the purpose of facilitating the restoration. The spirit of the project was captured in a simple yet elegant manner, without diminishing the Washington Monument's visibility or its importance as a cultural icon on the mall of the nation's capital.

*Commemorative print by Michael Graves*

## Competition for Peek & Cloppenburg Department Store

*Dusseldorf, Germany, 1998*

The competition entry for a department store for one of Germany's largest clothing companies reflects its dynamic urban surroundings and makes the internal retail displays visible to the passerby. The site, located on Schadowstrasse, the city's most prominent shopping street, is influenced by an adjacent elevated highway, the landmark Berliner Allee. Two glass pylons, one developed at the most prominent corner of the building and the other located directly across the street, form a prominent gateway in the city and provide a well-lit showcase for general merchandise and special promotions. This competition entry was not chosen for implementation.

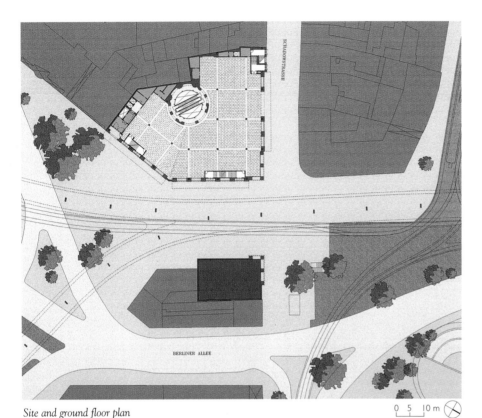

Site and ground floor plan

0  5  10 m

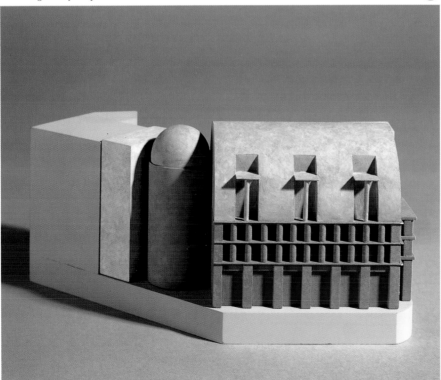

*Preliminary model view from Schadowstrasse*

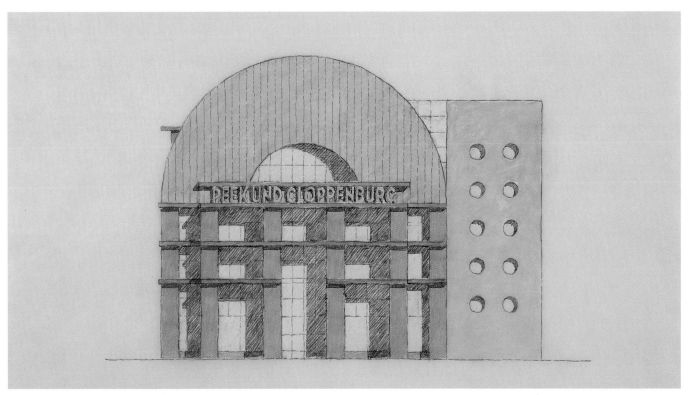

*Preliminary Berliner Allee elevation*

*Preliminary Schadowstrasse elevation*

*Model view from Berliner Allee*

*Night view from Schadowstrasse*

## Competition for the Main Library of Nashville and Davidson County

*Nashville, Tennessee, 1998*

1 Young adult collection
2 Children's library
3 Storytelling pavilion

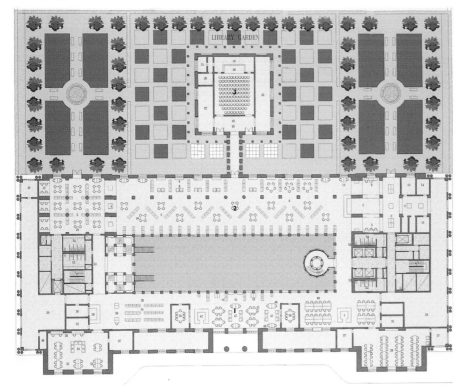

*Second floor plan*

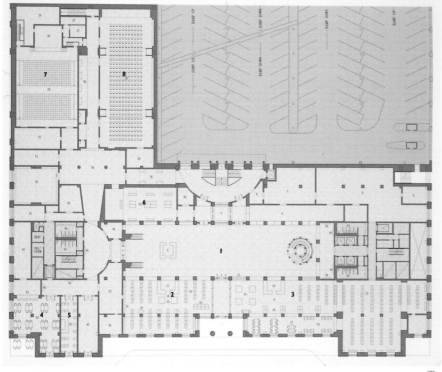

*Ground floor plan*

0  16  32 ft

The competition entry for Nashville's Main Library relates to its urban context, creates a dynamic and memorable public image, and provides special places for individual study and contemplation. The massing and entrance are organized symmetrically about the axis of Capitol Boulevard, which becomes an urban forecourt to the building, leading up to the Tennessee State Capitol.

Internally, the library is organized around two large public spaces, the Main Lobby and the Grand Reading Room, which are stacked above each other. Library-goers immediately encounter information and circulation desks in the lobby and gain views to the Children's Department on the second floor. The Children's Department opens onto the rooftop of an adjacent garage, developed as a garden containing a whimsical storytelling pavilion. The Grand Reading Room for the adult collections is organized around a two-story vaulted atrium connecting the fourth and fifth floors. The atrium's wooden columns and struts, along with warm wood detailing and paneling throughout the library, relate to the lore of this hilly, forested area of Tennessee, thus enhancing the public's identification with the region. This scheme was not selected for implementation.

1 Lobby
2 Audio-visual collection
3 Popular library
4 Café
5 Bookstore
6 Gallery
7 Auditorium
8 Multipurpose room

*Church Street elevation study*

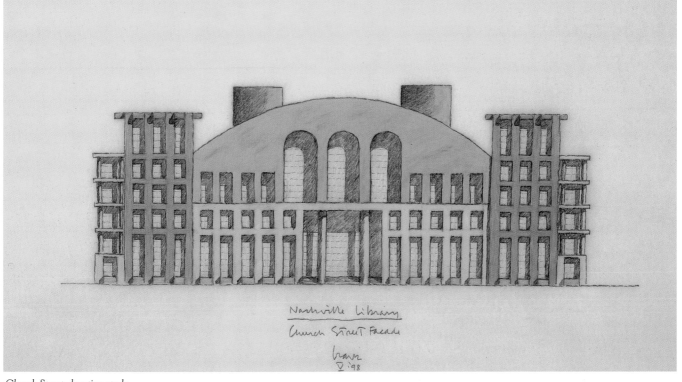

*Church Street elevation study*

Grand Reading Room

Lobby

Night view from Church Street

# St. Mary's Church

*Rockledge, Florida, 1998*

*View from the south*

St. Mary's Church, the parish church for a large congregation in central Florida, is located on a 40-acre site adjacent to a small school and convent. The program includes a 1200-seat main assembly space and a 130-seat daily chapel.

The design of the church, which comprises a series of elements along a linear axis, symbolizes the pilgrimage, an important metaphor in Catholic teaching. The site design further emphasizes the linear axis of the church, extending it beyond the building through an open-roofed space and along a processional way — an outdoor walk lined by the depictions of the Stations of the Cross. The several elements of the building are articulated as geometrically distinct forms enhanced by variations in color.

The main assembly gathers both the congregation and clergy into a single, circular space where all participate in the celebration of the mass, embodying the theology that the church is created by the active participation of all.

*Entrance elevation*

*Garden elevation*

*Main assembly*

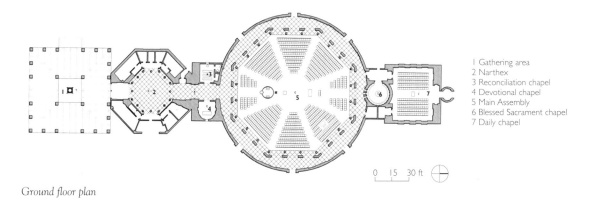

1 Gathering area
2 Narthex
3 Reconciliation chapel
4 Devotional chapel
5 Main Assembly
6 Blessed Sacrament chapel
7 Daily chapel

*Ground floor plan*

0   15   30 ft

# Private Residence

*Livingston, New Jersey, 1998*

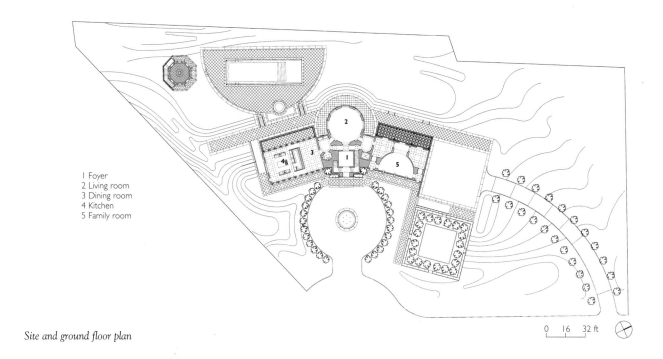

1 Foyer
2 Living room
3 Dining room
4 Kitchen
5 Family room

*Site and ground floor plan*

0  16  32 ft

This single-family house is sited on a hillside in northern New Jersey, which offers an expansive view of the landscape to the west. The extensive program is divided into three distinct sections connected horizontally and vertically by a three-story stair. The house is entered at the middle level on axis with a large rotunda containing the living room, a small gymnasium below and the master bedroom above.

The south wing, a light-filled pavilion distinguished by a row of two-story columns, contains the dining rooms and kitchen, bedrooms above and a small theater and family room below. The lower level opens onto stepped terraces, fountains and a swimming pool. In contrast, the north wing is more private, with offices and a second family room on the main floor, bedrooms upstairs, and guestrooms, storage and garages below.

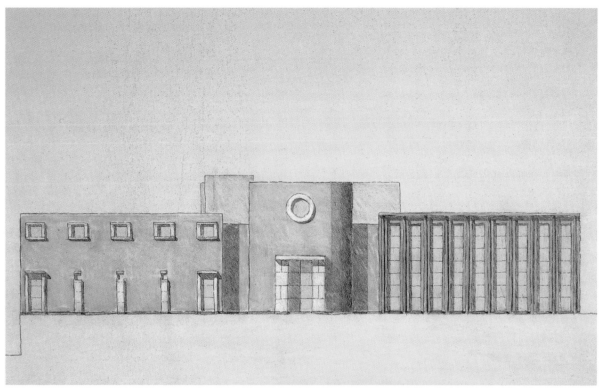

Entrance elevation

Garden elevation

## Martel, Jones and Brown Colleges Rice University

*Houston, Texas, 1998*

The master plan for Rice University's north campus includes construction of a new residential college, Martel College, and expansion of two neighboring 1970s-era colleges, Jones and Brown. Martel College is a self-contained 106,000-square-foot complex containing a 234-bed dormitory, classrooms and study areas, a library, apartments for residential advisors and visiting faculty, a house for the College Master and family, lounges and dining commons, and a kitchen and servery that provide central food preparation for all three colleges. The expansions of the other two colleges contain new dining rooms, additional living quarters, classrooms, a library for Brown, and a Master's House for Jones.

The planning strategy provides a clear identity for this area of the campus, which recalls the open residential courtyards and axial planning of Rice University's historic main campus designed around 1913 by Ralph Adams Cram and Bertram Goodhue. Similarly, the building facades and use of materials, especially the brickwork with its large horizontal joints, are compatible with the original campus buildings, yet also establish a fresh architectural character for the colleges.

*Martel College student residence wing*

194

*Top right: Martel College entrance*

*Bottom right: Martel College student
residence wing and entrance*

*Following pages: Martel College dining room*

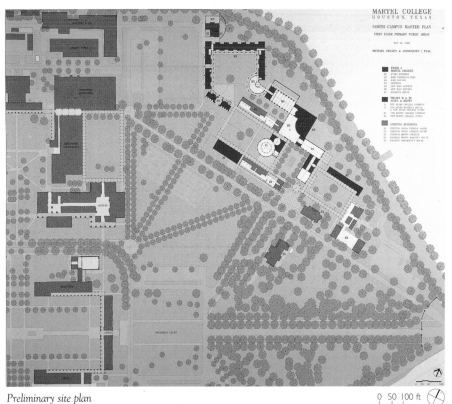

*Preliminary site plan*

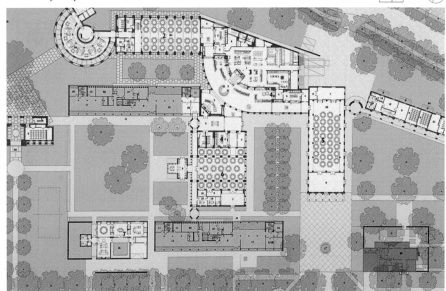

*Preliminary ground floor plan of new dining facilities*

1 Martel College lounge
2 Martel College commons
3 Central kitchen/servery
4 Satellite servery
5 Brown College commons and lounge
6 Jones College commons and lounge
7 Jones College master's house

Jones College expansion

Master's house

*Jones College dining room*

# JAL Plaza Prototype

*Japan, 1998*

*Scheme B entrance elevation*

JAL Plaza is a prototype intended for development in various suburban locations throughout Japan. A large-scale shopping mall is organized around a public galleria at the center of the building. Located to one side of the mall is a 200-room wedding hotel with extensive banquet facilities. An entertainment center anchors the other end of the building and includes movie theaters, bowling alleys, pachinko parlors and a spa. The massing and facades of the three parts of the program are given distinctive identities in order to create an image that would be recognizable from location to location.

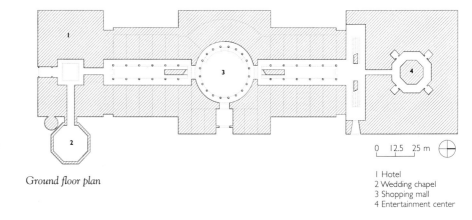

*Ground floor plan*

0    12.5    25 m

1 Hotel
2 Wedding chapel
3 Shopping mall
4 Entertainment center

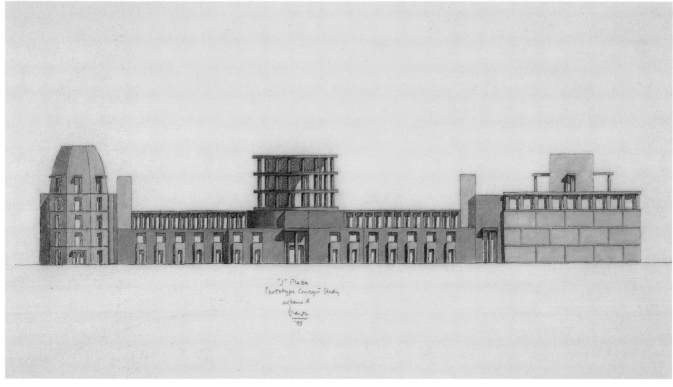

*Scheme A entrance elevation*

## Resort Hotel at Cotton Bay

*Eleuthera, Bahamas, 1998*

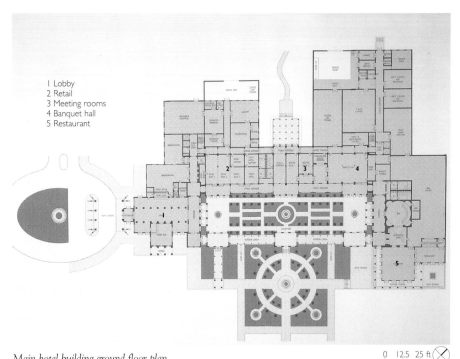

1 Lobby
2 Retail
3 Meeting rooms
4 Banquet hall
5 Restaurant

*Main hotel building ground floor plan*

0  12.5  25 ft

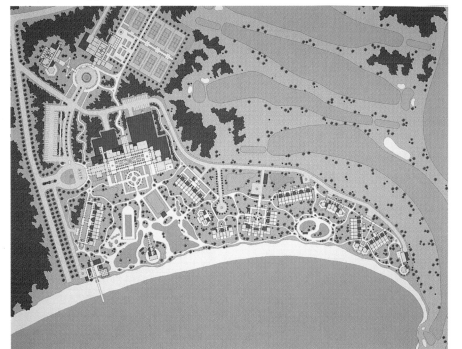

*Site plan*

0  50  100 ft

The design of the resort hotel at Cotton Bay emphasizes the relationship between buildings and the landscape, including the bay and the adjacent golf course. The hotel is composed as a series of individual buildings oriented toward the bay, and incorporates numerous landscape features such as pools and gardens. The 64-room U-shaped main building is organized around a formal landscaped courtyard onto which face various public facilities such as the bar, restaurants and banquet hall. Seven stories of guest rooms are organized in a single-loaded corridor configuration that allows water views from every room. The remaining guestrooms are accommodated in two arc-shaped buildings centered on a landscaped swimming pool and the beach.

Throughout the resort, the buildings are given a quiet elegance resulting from a combination of traditional architectural character and vernacular associations. The facades are clad in whitewashed rough stone accented with wood treillage, shutters and louvers. To complement the simple nature of the buildings, the landscaping creates an informal, natural tropical environment of indigenous vegetation such as palm trees, climbing vines and flowers.

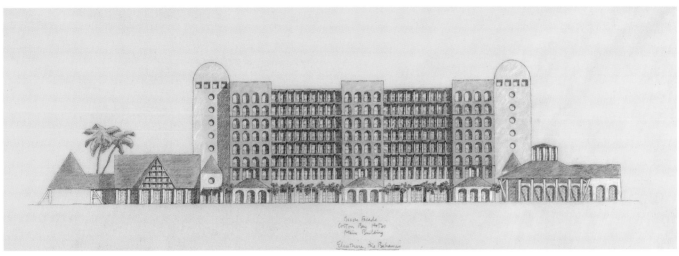

*Main hotel building elevation*

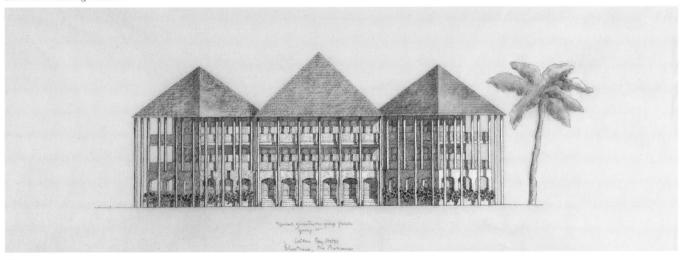

*Guestroom group beachfront elevation*

*Bar and restaurant beachfront elevation*

# Cedar Gables

*Minnetonka, Minnesota, 1998*

*Street facade*

Cedar Gables is a house designed for the 1999 Parade of Homes show house tour in the Minneapolis area. Its name refers to the distinctive symmetrical three-gabled cedar-shingled roof forms. The windows are framed with deep trim, and the roof and second floor overhang the main level, creating shadows and strong forms and massing that distinguish this house within its suburban neighborhood.

Cedar Gables has 4,300 square feet of living space on two levels, a three-car garage and a walk-out basement. The plan features a centrally located double-height stair hall that opens up the middle of the house. A two-story, maple-paneled Great Room adjoins an eat-in kitchen with a deck overlooking a pond.

The interiors of the house incorporate many elements designed by Graves, including lighting fixtures, plumbing fixtures and fittings, carpets and door and drapery hardware. The house was furnished with numerous items of indoor and outdoor furniture, framed art, housewares and decorative accessories designed for Target Stores.

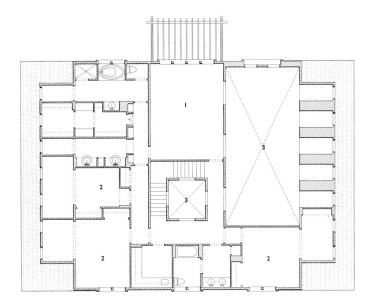

1 Master bedroom
2 Bedroom
3 Open to below

*Second floor plan*

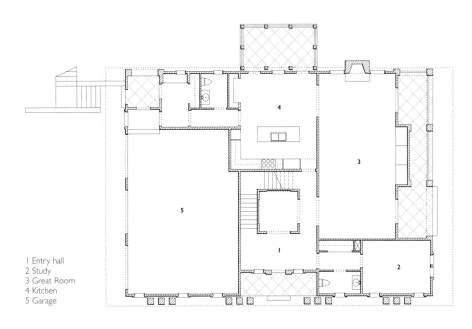

1 Entry hall
2 Study
3 Great Room
4 Kitchen
5 Garage

*Ground floor plan*

0   5   10 ft

Kitchen

Master bedroom

# Lotus Hotel and Convention Center

*26th of October City (Cairo), Egypt, 1998*

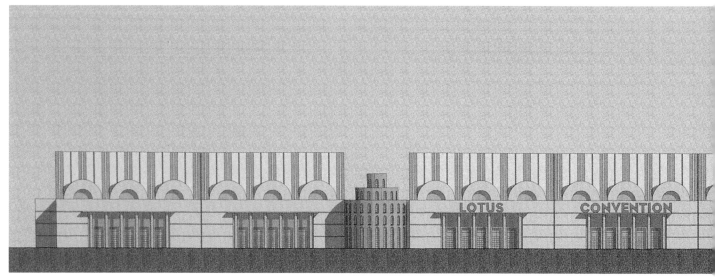

*Convention center and hotel street elevation*

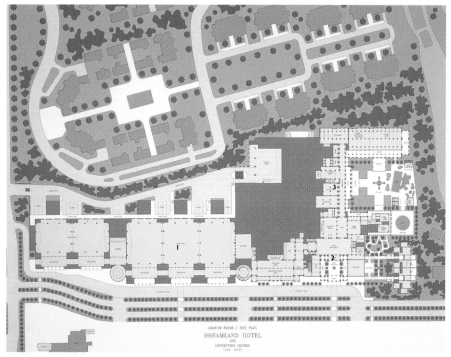

*Site and ground floor plan*

1 Convention Center
2 Conference Hall
3 Hotel

The Lotus Hotel and Convention Center is sited in a larger development in 26th of October City, a new city outside Cairo. The project is planned for phased construction, necessitating organizing the major components on separate footprints adjacent to each other. One phase, facing the golf course, consists of a 550-room business hotel and a series of multi-unit condominium villas. In subsequent phases, a convention center is planned to extend along a major public street. Included in the program are two banquet halls, a 15,000-square-meter exhibition hall and meetings rooms. The project is intended to be international and urban in character but still make reference to its Egyptian location through facade details, materials and colors.

*Hotel courtyard elevation*

*Beachfront elevation*

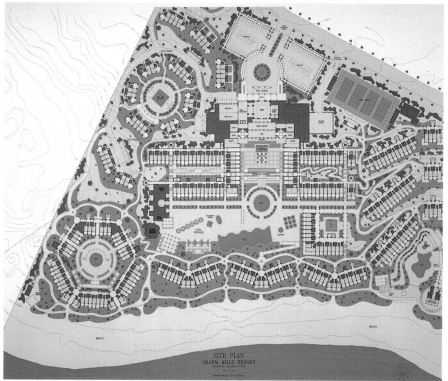

*Site and ground floor plan*

The Sharm Hills Resort, located on the waterfront in Sharm el Sheikh at the southernmost point of the Sinai Peninsula, is a 48,000-square-meter hotel development with approximately 400 conventional and time-share guest rooms and 54 individual cottages. Supporting facilities include restaurants, retail shops, a health club and an aquatic center.

The site's rocky, arid landscape slopes steeply to the water's edge. The main hotel building is sited at the top of the slope and smaller scale guestroom clusters are developed close to the beach, taking advantage of the terrain to maximize views toward the water. The character of the resort in form, materials and coloration was intended to reflect local vernacular architecture and building techniques.

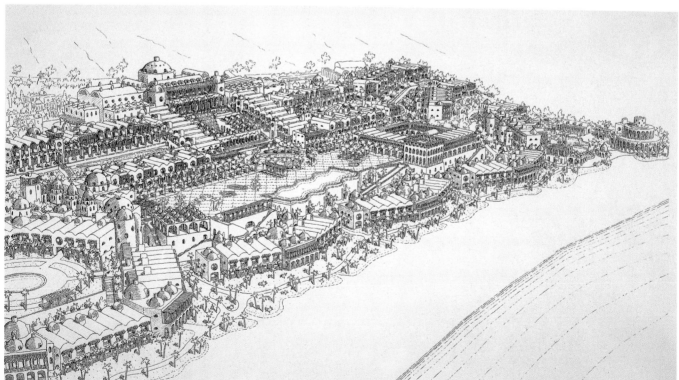

*Aerial view of the resort*

# Competition for the National Bank of Abu Dhabi

*Abu Dhabi, U.A.E., 1998*

The proposed headquarters of the National Bank of Abu Dhabi occupies a prominent site that anchors a line of modern commercial buildings on both sides of Sheikh Khalifa Bin Zahed Street at the intersection of Lulu Street. The site has views to both the Al Asima Public Gardens to the east across Lulu Street and the Arabian Gulf approximately 500 meters to the north beyond the Corniche Road.

This competition entry, which was not chosen for development, combines contemporary tall building technology with the aesthetic sense of traditional Islamic masonry architecture. The 25-story tower contains the main branch of the National Bank on five floors within the base of the building, and offices for the bank and tenants on the upper floors. The bank's executive offices are located in the penthouse. A multipurpose reception hall is located at the top of the building, adjacent to which a double-height exterior court with an open-air oculus and palm trees provides an unexpected gardenlike space with a spectacular view of the Arabian Gulf.

*Palm court*

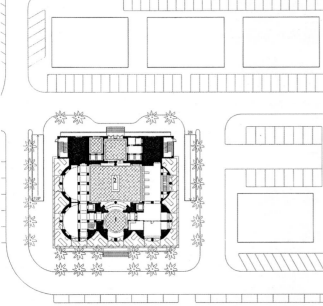

1 Lobby
2 Banking hall

*Site and ground floor plan*

0 5 10 m

# The NovaCare Complex
# Philadelphia Eagles
# Training Center

*Philadelphia, Pennsylvania, 1998*

The NovaCare Complex, a training center for the Philadelphia Eagles football team, is located on the site of a former Naval Hospital near the stadium in Philadelphia. The L-shaped building contains a two-story office wing and a one-story athletic wing. The entrance to the office wing is flanked by large-scale team emblems. The athletic wing contains high-end locker rooms, a dining hall for the players, an executive dining room, a video room and a television and radio production facility. This wing, with its vaulted roof reminiscent of traditional athletic field houses, faces outdoor practice fields located on the site. The project also includes an indoor practice field in a separate structure.

*View from the practice field*

1 Lobby
2 Cafeteria
3 Executive dining room
4 Auditorium
5 Locker room
6 Weight room

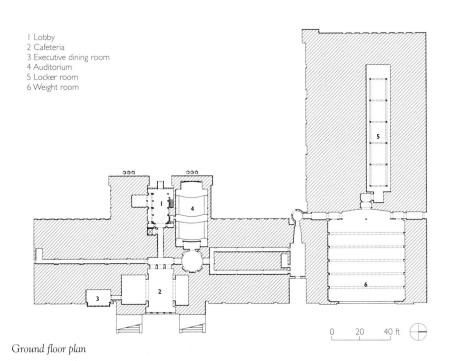

*Ground floor plan*

0   20   40 ft

*Entrance facade*

Boardroom

Weight room

*Auditorium*

*Locker room*

# Philadelphia Eagles
# Football Stadium Study

*Philadelphia, Pennsylvania, 1999*

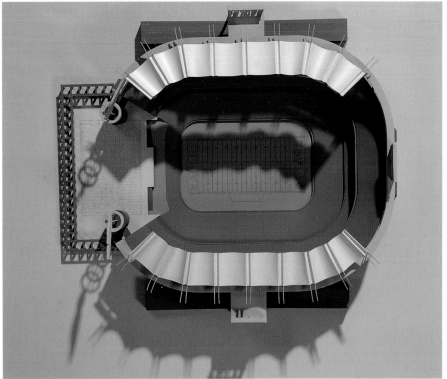

*Overhead view of stadium model*

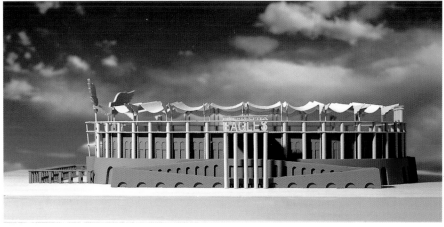

*Model view of stadium entrance facade*

Located on Broad and Pattison Streets in Philadelphia, this open-bowl 60,000-seat stadium is designed primarily for football. The scheme creates an important public space in front of the stadium, as the beginning of a procession through the concourse to the seating. By locating the various program elements at one end of the stadium and organizing them in section, the concourse is opened up to the field. Spectators walking along the concourse thus always have a view of the field.

*Perspective view of entrance and stadium*

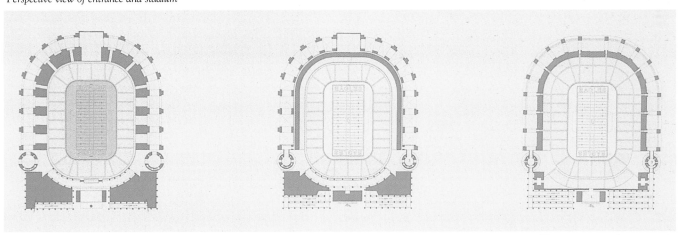

*Lower concourse plan*                *Box and suite level plan*                *Upper concourse plan*

# Target Stage
## at Harriet Island Park

*St. Paul, Minnesota, 1999*

*Target Stage*

Target Stage is located in a public park on Harriet Island and accommodates a variety of events, including graduations and various other seasonal community events, weddings, dance recitals, school plays, readings and concerts. It was also designed to be suitable for use by the Minnesota Orchestra and other major regional performance groups.

The park commission wanted the stage structure to be whimsical, transparent and ephemeral. The resulting design is a lacy, open steel structure that refers to the truss work of the bridges crossing the river and the industrial landscape that is part of the history of Saint Paul's riverfront.

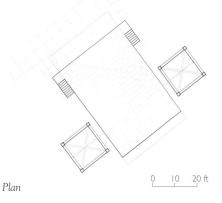

*Plan*

0   10   20 ft

226

# Elephant Fountain
at Target House

*Memphis, Tennessee, 1999*

*Elephant fountain*

*Elephant fountain study*

Target House is a residential building at St. Jude Children's Research Hospital where families, whose terminally ill children are undergoing long-term treatment, can assume as normal a family life as possible. In 1999, various personalities affiliated with Target either sponsored or designed facilities for Target House. The Michael Graves project is a large fountain located in a forecourt at the building entrance.

The fountain features four families of elephants made of copper and hammered to resemble topiary designed in collaboration with the sculptor Charlie Smith. Elephants were chosen as a theme since they are a symbol of luck and stand for the healing power of families. The fountain, designed by Hobbs Architectural Fountains is elaborately programmed with variations in water activity from multiple perimeter and central jets and from the elephants themselves. There is also a disk at child height that can be pushed to initiate a water sequence, creating an interactive environment.

Watch Technicum

*Lancaster County, Pennsylvania, 1999*

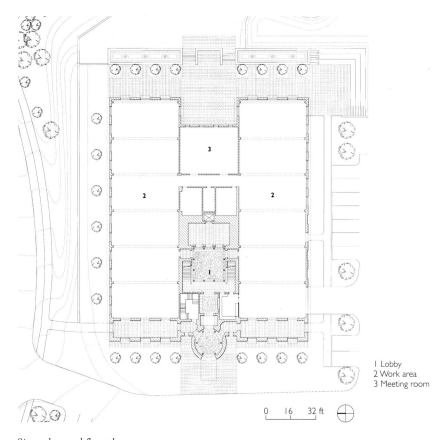

*Site and ground floor plan*

1 Lobby
2 Work area
3 Meeting room

0   16   32 ft

This 45,000-square-foot watch-making and service center is occupied by one of the most prestigious watch companies in the world. The fieldstone building complex with its barn motif provides a contextual interpretation of its Pennsylvania Dutch setting.

The dramatic entrance lobby features exposed timber truss work that is also reminiscent of the agricultural locale and Amish presence. Extensive site landscaping is accented by natural stone and completed by an outdoor seating area and pond with fountain.

Competition for the
Singapore National Library

*Singapore, 1999*

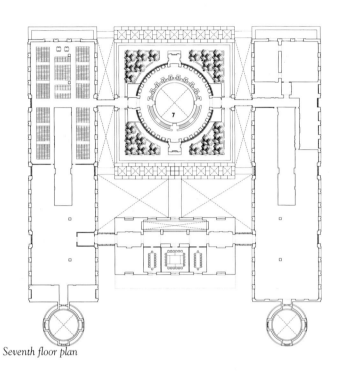

*Seventh floor plan*

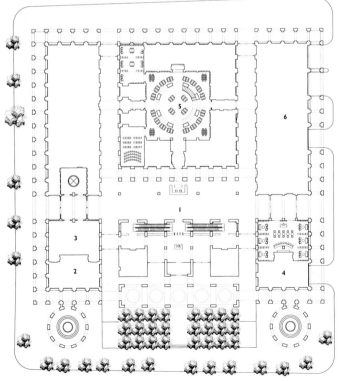

The program for the Singapore National Library comprises four discrete library departments separated by skylit internal "streets" connected above ground level by bridges. These passages visually and physically connect the departments and recall Singapore's traditional arcade-lined streets. The passages also help break up the potentially large floor plates and provide identity to the individual departments.

The plan and massing attempt to be as clear as possible so that the building can be readily understood by the public and easily administered by the staff. The two largest and most heavily used departments, the Lending Library and the Heritage Library, are centrally positioned to facilitate access and, in the case of the Heritage Reading Room, to offer views of the city.

The library's primary public entrance is located on Victoria Street adjacent to a tree-lined plaza defined by corner turrets and a covered arcade. Local materials such as limestone or sandstone used for the facades and flooring identify the library as specific to Singapore while the copper-clad parabolic roofs and rotundas effectively mark the building on the skyline. This competition entry was not selected for further development.

1 Lobby
2 Multipurpose room
3 Gallery
4 Gift shop and café
5 Reference library
6 Service
7 Heritage Library
  reading room

*Ground floor plan*

0  4  8 m

Heritage Reading Room

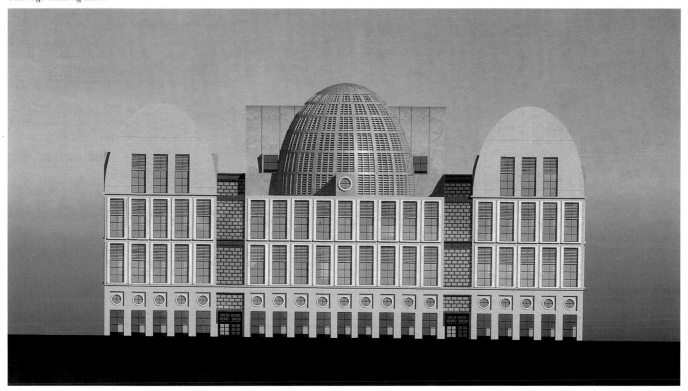

Victoria Street elevation

235

## Private Residence

*Lake Geneva, Switzerland, 1999*

The site for this private residence slopes steeply from the road to Lake Geneva. The entrance driveway creates a forecourt to a formal public facade facing the road; whereas, the water side of the house is informal and picturesque. Two wings that flank a central rotunda in the main body of the house and a parallel barrel-vaulted garden pavilion form a rear courtyard. Attached to the house, the kitchen occupies its own single-story wing with a rooftop terrace surrounded by a pergola.

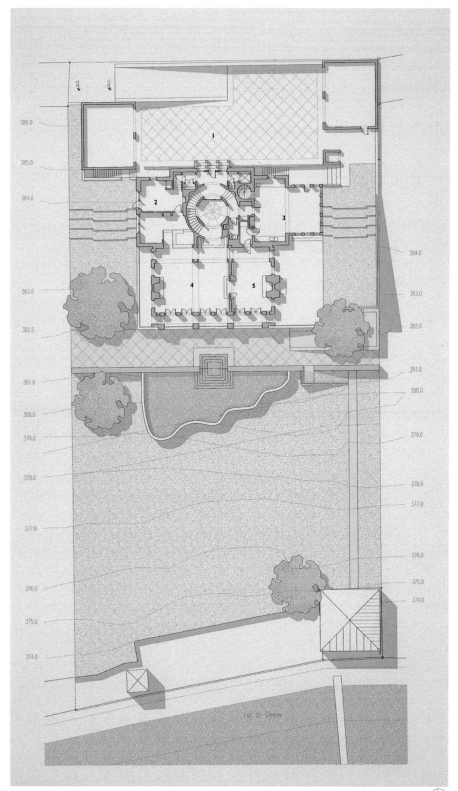

1 Entry court
2 Study
3 Kitchen
4 Living room
5 Dining room

*Site and ground floor plan*

0    2    4 m

Entrance elevation

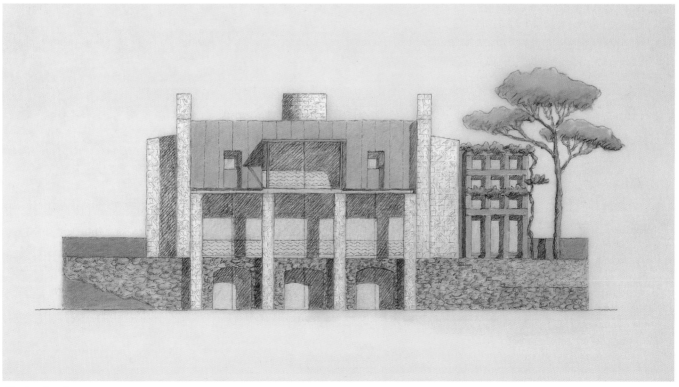

Garden elevation

# The Detroit Institute of Arts

*Detroit, Michigan, 1999*

The approximately 600,000-square-foot building complex of the Detroit Institute of Arts encompasses a historic building designed by Paul Cret and completed in 1927, and two modern additions completed in 1966 and 1971.

The main architectural goals of the renovation and expansion project depicted here are to improve the vertical and horizontal public circulation and thus make the visitor experience more legible, to increase the size and flexibility of the permanent and temporary exhibit galleries, to expand the educational center and museum shop, and to consolidate and upgrade food service facilities.

Circulation and orientation in the museum are greatly improved by the introduction of a significant new north-south passageway on the Woodward Avenue edge of the museum, punctuated with new public stairways that allow natural light into the passageway at both ends. As part of the renovation, the deteriorating facades of the modern wings are replaced in a manner compatible with Cret's design in composition, materials and color. A 40,000-square-foot addition for future galleries on the east side of the south wing provides temporary swing space for phasing construction in order to keep the museum operating and open to the public.

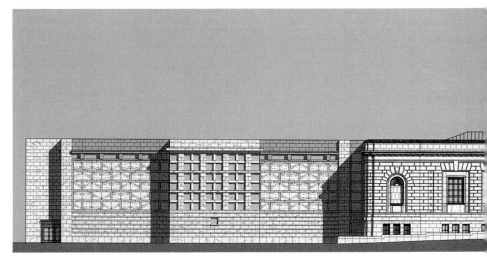

*Woodward Avenue elevation*

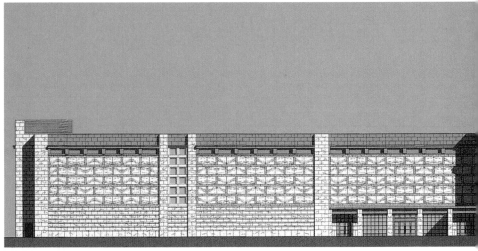

*John R. Street elevation*

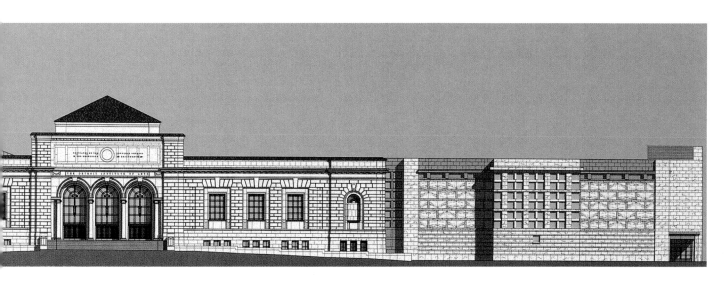

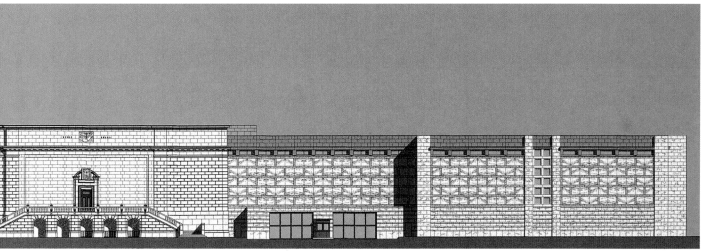

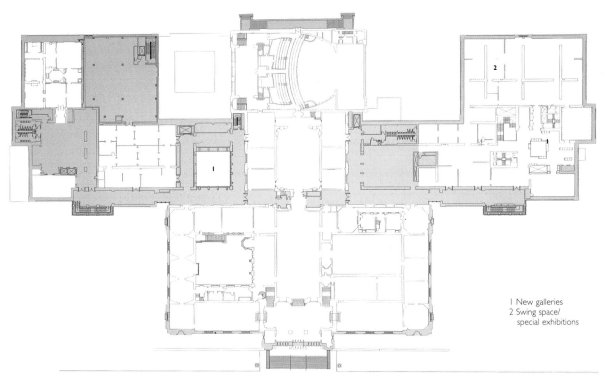

1 New galleries
2 Swing space/
  special exhibitions

*Main floor plan with alterations shaded*

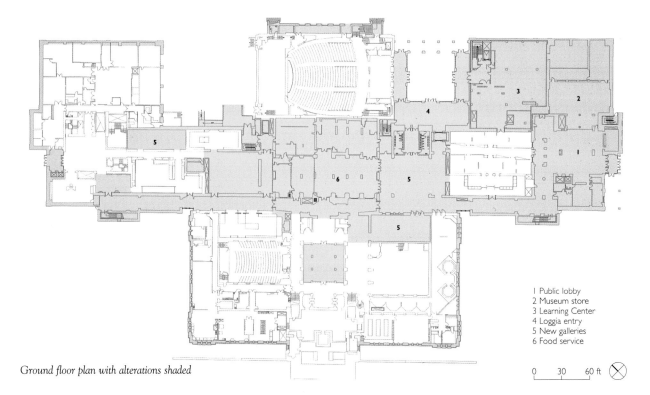

1 Public lobby
2 Museum store
3 Learning Center
4 Loggia entry
5 New galleries
6 Food service

*Ground floor plan with alterations shaded*

0    30    60 ft

*Dining room*

# Museum of the Shenandoah Valley

*Winchester, Virginia, 1999*

The Museum of the Shenandoah Valley is a new institution located on the grounds of the historic Glen Burnie estate in Winchester, Virginia, which contains 25 acres of gardens and the house of Winchester's founder, James Wood. The house is furnished with the decorative and fine arts collections of Wood's descendant, Julian Wood Glass, Jr., and is open to the public.

The design of the museum establishes its own identity within its historic context, reflecting the character of traditional local architecture, ranging from manor houses to farm buildings. The overall theme of the museum is "making a home in the Shenandoah Valley." The exhibits focus on furniture and decorative arts of the Shenandoah Valley, providing a rich context for visitors to see Glen Burnie's historic house, collections and gardens.

*Entrance elevation*

*Side elevation*

242

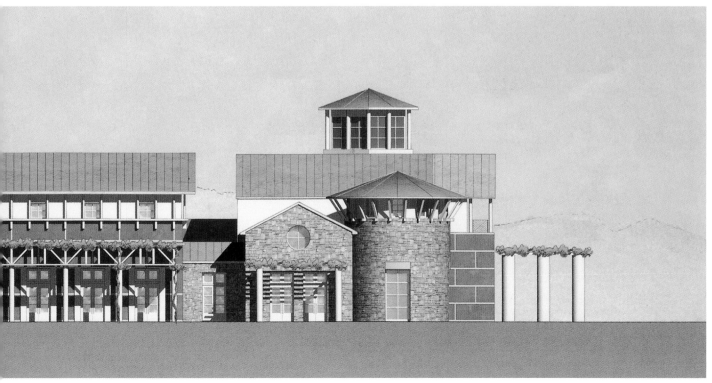

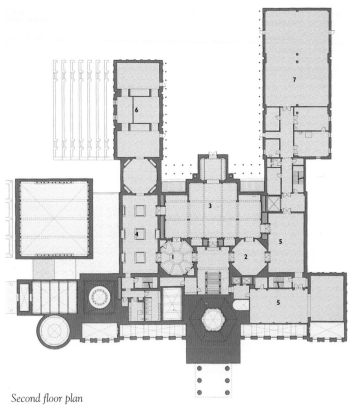

Second floor plan

1 Lobby
2 Learning Center
3 Research center
4 Museum store
5 Tearoom
6 Prefunction
7 Reception all

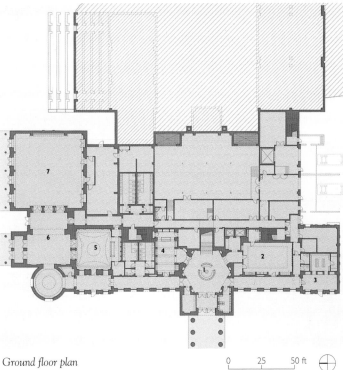

Ground floor plan

1 Orientation gallery
2 Miniatures gallery
3 Shenandoah Valley gallery
4 Decorative Arts gallery
5 Changing exhibitions gallery
6 Julian Wood Glass, Jr. galleries
7 Collections storage

0    25    50 ft

Model view looking toward the entrance

Glen Burnie historic house

# Cosmotoda Master Plan

*Barcelona, Spain, 1999*

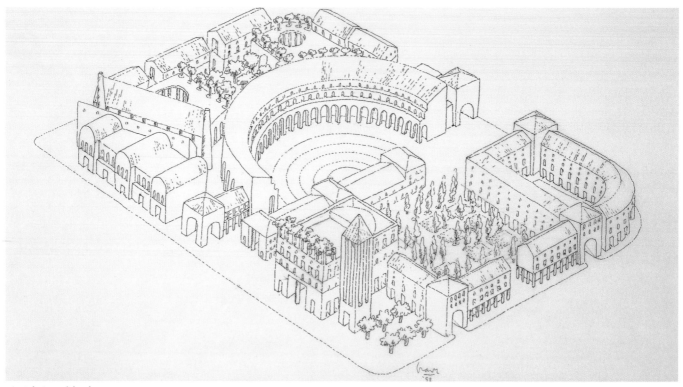

*Aerial view of development*

The Master Plan for the block in l'Hospitalet bounded by Avenida Enric Prat de la Riba, Josep Tarradellas i Joan, Carrer Canigo and Carrer Batllori proposes an exciting new residential and retail project that is intended to be a catalyst for neighboring developments.

The plan for new construction accommodates several existing structures, including a seven-story automobile dealership and a four-story former factory. The urban planning approach is characteristic of the city's traditional land-use patterns, in that the new buildings are positioned both to reinforce the edges of the surrounding streets and to define a series of figural, axially connected outdoor spaces in the center. Typical of Barcelona, entries to the block occur at the street intersections and also along the length of surrounding streets.

The existing factory building, located in the approximate center of the block, is proposed for future conversion to a cultural facility serving the community. To the east and west of the factory, two large-scaled landscaped garden plazas integrate this building with adjacent structures. Programmatically, the new buildings comprise two floors of retail and three floors of housing. The retail levels are articulated with pedestrian-scaled entrances and arcades, which provide vitality at the street level. Variety in the massing of the upper levels and roofs of the buildings create opportunities for creating roof terraces for the residences. The range of forms and articulation of small-scale details impart a sense of domestic life to this project in keeping with the character of the traditional sections of l'Hospitalet and Barcelona.

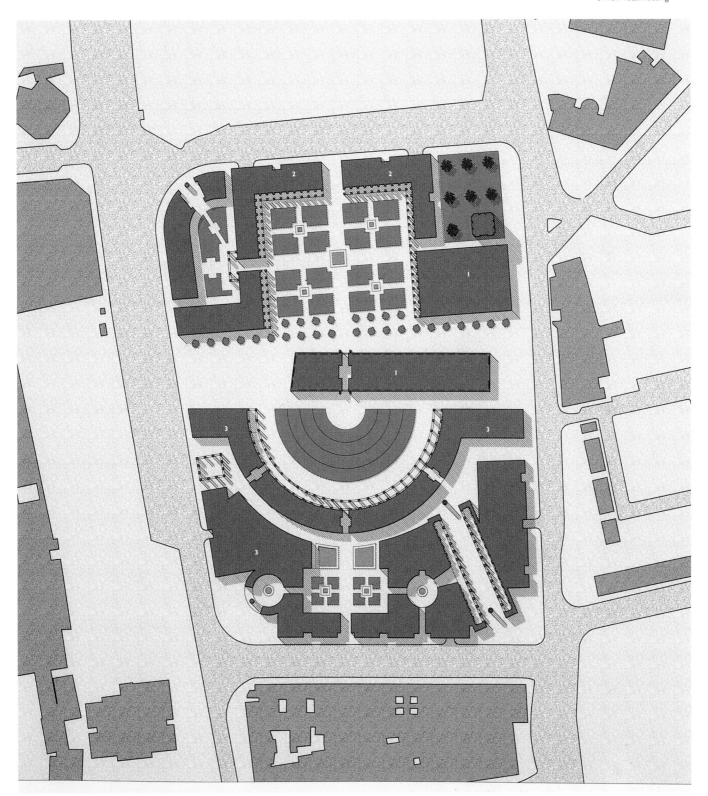

1 Existing building
2 New housing
3 New retail/housing

*Site plan*

0   12.5   25 m

## 425 Fifth Avenue

*New York, New York, 2000*

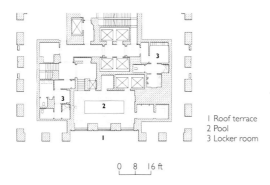

1 Roof terrace
2 Pool
3 Locker room

0  8  16 ft

*Seventh floor plan*

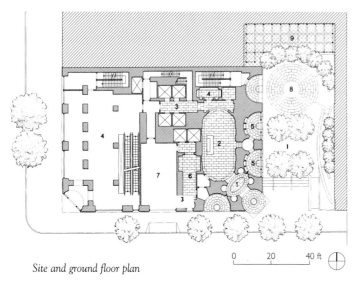

1 Plaza and garden
2 Residential lobby
3 Office lobby
4 Retail

0  20  40 ft

*Site and ground floor plan*

*Residential lobby*

This mixed-use tower rising to a height equivalent to 67 stories is located on the northeast corner of Fifth Avenue and 38th Street. Its massing reconciles New York City zoning regulations and the relatively small footprint of the site by placing a thin residential tower with setbacks on a six-story commercial base.

The scale, detailing and materials of the base of 425 Fifth Avenue complement historically significant buildings in the neighborhood and are reminiscent of traditional New York towers. The base contains two floors of retail and four floors of offices. The amenities for the residences are concentrated in the Fifth Avenue Club, which occupies the seventh and eighth floors. A major public terrace wraps around the building on the seventh floor. The eighth floor contains an extensive business center and the lounge for the Envoy Club, an extended-stay residence that rises through six floors. Upper-level apartments and condominiums feature a variety of studio, one-, two- and three-bedroom units, which offer protected views of uptown and downtown Manhattan, including an excellent view of the nearby Empire State Building.

*View from Fifth Avenue and 38th Street*

*Facing page: View from the city*

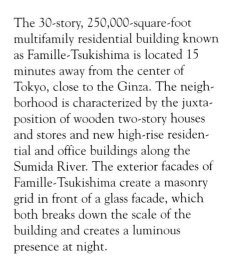

## Famille-Tsukishima

*Tokyo, Japan, 2000*

The 30-story, 250,000-square-foot multifamily residential building known as Famille-Tsukishima is located 15 minutes away from the center of Tokyo, close to the Ginza. The neighborhood is characterized by the juxtaposition of wooden two-story houses and stores and new high-rise residential and office buildings along the Sumida River. The exterior facades of Famille-Tsukishima create a masonry grid in front of a glass facade, which both breaks down the scale of the building and creates a luminous presence at night.

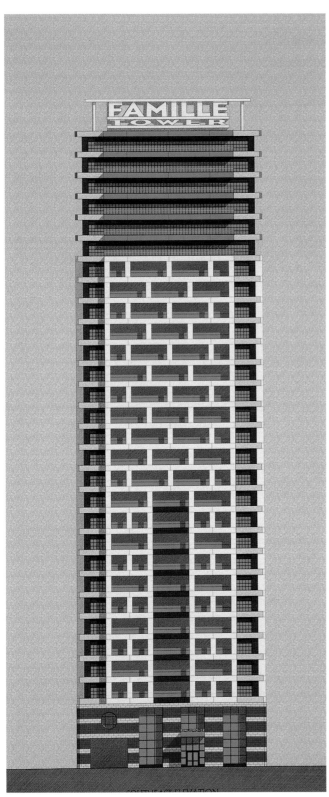

*Primary elevation*

# Hart Productions Studio

*San Francisco, California, 2000*

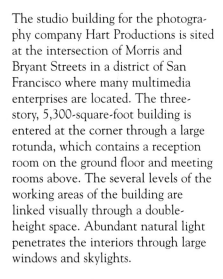

Morris Street elevation

Third floor plan

Second floor plan

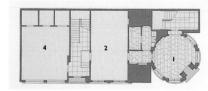

Ground floor plan

0   8   16 ft

1 Lobby/reception
2 Studio
3 Meeting Room
4 Garage
5 Open to below

The studio building for the photography company Hart Productions is sited at the intersection of Morris and Bryant Streets in a district of San Francisco where many multimedia enterprises are located. The three-story, 5,300-square-foot building is entered at the corner through a large rotunda, which contains a reception room on the ground floor and meeting rooms above. The several levels of the working areas of the building are linked visually through a double-height space. Abundant natural light penetrates the interiors through large windows and skylights.

The simple massing of the building is sympathetic to the prevailing context of industrial buildings, whereas the lively coloration and articulation of the facades announce the artistic purpose of the studio.

# Tallahassee Community Hospital

*Tallahassee, Florida, 2000*

*View toward the entrance*

The Community Hospital in Tallahassee is an eight-story replacement facility for Columbia ACH. Located on a prominent urban site, the hospital is envisioned to have a civic presence appropriate to its prominence in the community. The Tennessee-based firm, Thomas, Miller & Partners, planned the building technically and enlisted Graves' participation to develop the exterior character and the public interiors.

By emphasizing the entrance portico and central pavilion, the hospital is given a human scale and sense of accessibility. Taking cues from the design of hotel buildings, the entrance sequence and lobbies are given a comfortable, non-institutional character to improve the hospital experience for patients and their families.

# Private Offices

*Washington, D.C., 2000*

*Reception*

The corridors of this suite of executive offices and conference rooms double as a library in order to enliven them and break down the scale of their lengthy elevations. Glass doors to perimeter offices allow daylight to penetrate the interior. The stained maple millwork and stone floor patterns provide a streetlike rhythm and richness. The main conference room, while equipped with sophisticated technical systems, is given a domestic character through its finishes, custom furnishings and artwork.

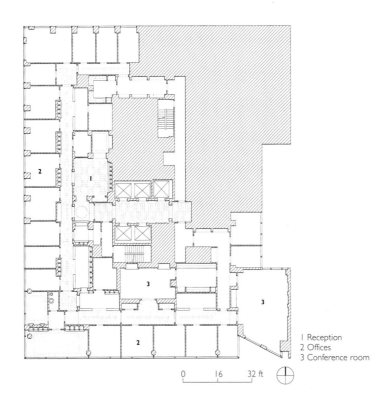

1 Reception
2 Offices
3 Conference room

*Floor plan*

0    16    32 ft

Executive office

Main conference room

# Sportevo

*North Charleston, South Carolina, 2000*

Sportevo is a prototype for a series of
family-friendly sports complexes that
cater to fitness and activity needs of
every age group. Each Sportevo center
would contain general recreational
facilities as well as venues for sports
that are most popular in its particular
geographic area, such as golf and tennis facilities and indoor rinks for soccer
and in-line skating. A variety of eating
establishments and retail shops make
Sportevo an all-day destination for
families. A consistent upbeat identity
is provided by large-scale graphics and
bold patterns and colors applied to the
expansive building surfaces.

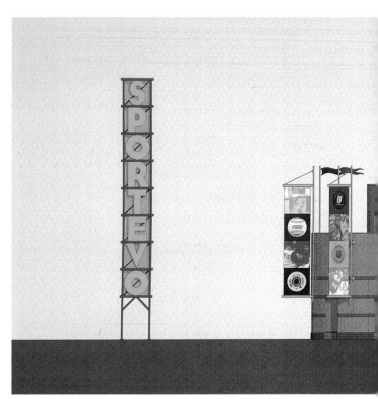

*Sportevo retail center*

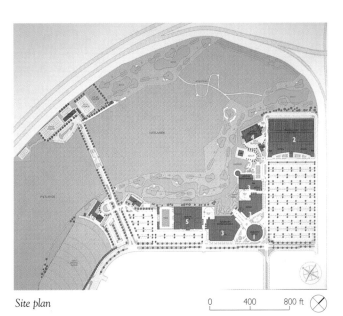

*Site plan*

0     400     800 ft

1 Retail center
2 Performance center
3 Retail
4 XPLEX
5 Life center
6 Golf center
7 Tennis center

*Sportevo performance center*

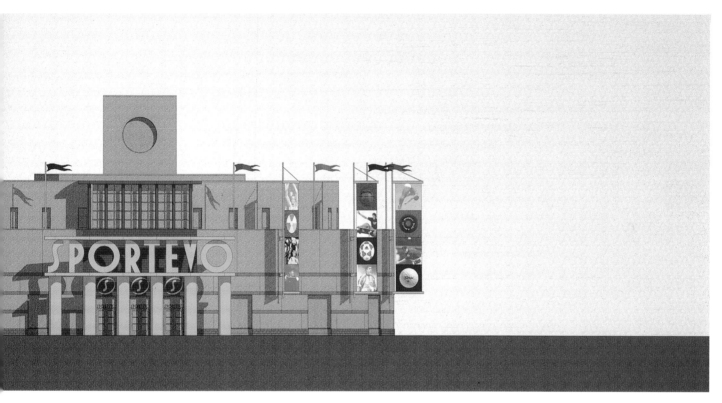

# Stoa Olympica

*Maroussi (Athens), Greece, 2000*

*Entrance elevation of retail center and office buildings*

The selection of Athens as the site for the 2004 Olympic Games created opportunities for significant investment in the local infrastructure and facilities associated with the Games. Consequently, new locations for real estate development emerged in places such as Maroussi, a municipality northeast of Athens where the Olympic Stadium and other sport facilities are located. The site for the mixed-use development known as Stoa Olympica forms a link between the northern and eastern expansion of the municipal transportation system and the central part of the city. It therefore has the capacity to draw large numbers of people.

The program for the development includes 64,000 square meters of retail and entertainment facilities, 15,000 square meters of offices, and parking for 3,400 cars. The retail center is organized on several levels as an indoor-outdoor environment. In addition, a master plan was prepared for extensive residential development on an adjacent site.

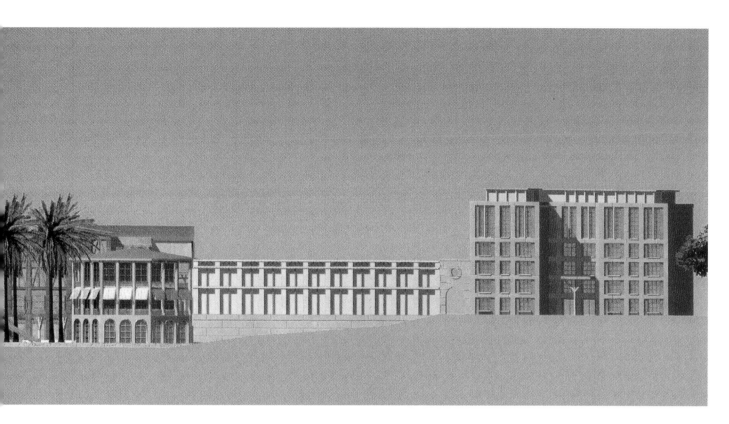

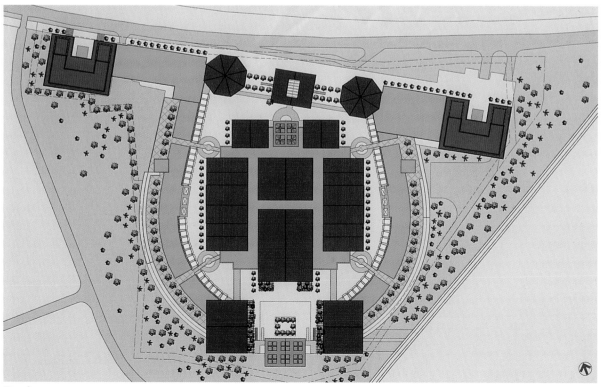

*Site plan*

*Retail center entrance*

*Cinema complex*

*Retail arcade*

*Cinema complex and food courts*

# Piazza Duomo
# and Piazza Orsini

*Benevento, Italy, 2000*

1 Proposed museum
2 Piazza Duomo
3 Existing church
4 Proposed hypostyle hall
   in Piazza Orsini

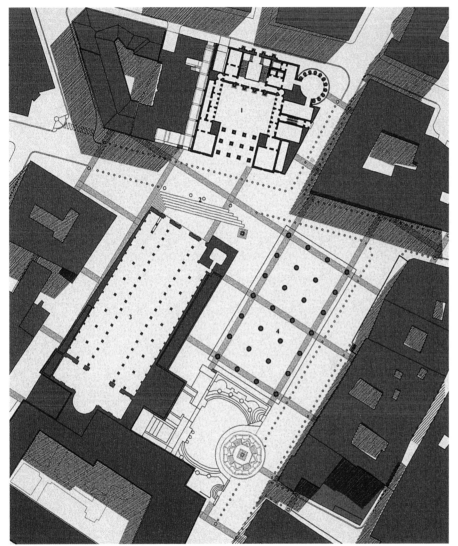

*Site and ground floor plan*

*Referential sketches of Roman ruins*

An international consultation was held to revise the urban plan of Piazza Duomo and Piazza Orsini in Benevento and to design a new museum. This proposal to treat the combined *piazze* as a precinct binds together these disparate urban sites while preserving their individuality. The *piazze* become more cohesive by strengthening the figural character of the open space and articulating the entire ground plane as a large-scale grid.

The location of Corso Garibaldi in Piazza Duomo immediately in front of the church creates a paradoxical urban condition in that one would normally expect a forecourt in that location. Thus, despite its name, there is in effect no defined piazza. The new museum is sited immediately opposite the church, completing the streetwall along Corso Garibaldi and creating a civic presence appropriate to the institution and its urban position. The museum is organized around an open-air courtyard, which can be thought of as an internalized forecourt for the church.

While the northern edge of Corso Garibaldi is seen as a continuous streetwall, the southern edge leading into Piazza Orsini is more informal and reflects a shift from the orthogonal of the street to the diagonal of the church. A new building is proposed for Piazza Orsini, a hypostyle hall reminiscent of market structures seen throughout Italy. While open-air, the hall has a volumetric presence sympathetic to that of the church and yet provides visibility and pedestrian circulation at the ground level.

*Museum view from the hypostyle hall*

*Hypostyle hall*

# Private Museum in the Middle East

*2000*

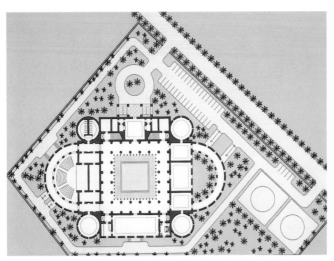

*Scheme 1 ground floor plan*

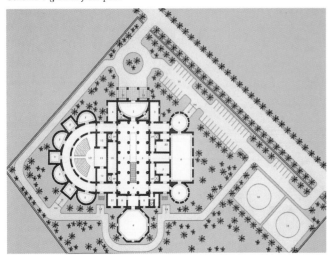

*Scheme 2 ground floor plam*

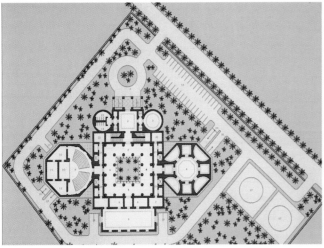

*Scheme 3 ground floor plan*

0  10  20 m

Three alternative conceptual designs were prepared for a speculative private museum and exhibition center to be located in the Middle East. The 15,000-square-meter program to be developed on three levels includes a major exhibition hall, galleries for a permanent collection of art and artifacts, a multipurpose theater, a reception hall, offices, private library, storage and support facilities. The architectural character of each of the schemes was intended to relate to the indigenous architecture of the region.

*Scheme 1 elevation*

*Scheme 2 elevation*

*Scheme 3 elevation*

267

# Private Villa Compound in the Middle East

*2000*

A conceptual design was prepared for a private villa compound accommodating several related individuals and their families. The compound is oriented toward a body of water and includes common recreational facilities as well as private residences for each family. At the owners' request, the compound has an architectural character reminiscent of traditional buildings found in the Mediterranean region.

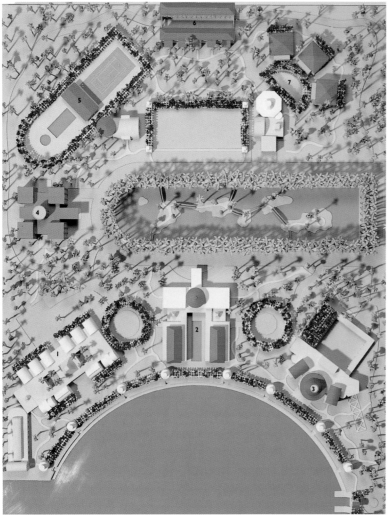

*Site model*

1 Villa 1
2 Majlis
3 Villa 2
4 Guest house
5 Swimming/tennis
6 Service
7 Wives' residences

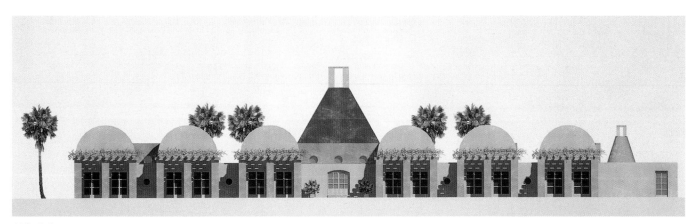

*Villa 1 elevation*

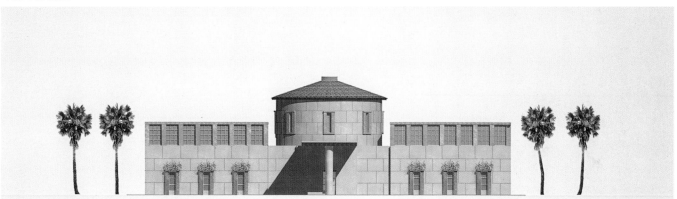

*Majlis elevation*

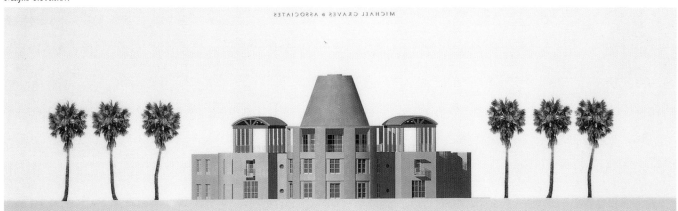

*Villa 2 elevation*

# Houston Branch of the Federal Reserve Bank of Dallas

*Houston, Texas, 2000*

By drawing on the traditions of national bank buildings throughout the country and the architecture of the Southwest, this new building is intended to be easily identifiable as the "Houston Fed." In order to communicate the civic importance of the Federal Reserve Bank as a national financial institution, the design is intentionally timeless and conveys permanence and authority balanced with openness. By using local materials and colors, as well as loggias, terraces and pergolas typical of Houston architecture, the character is also rooted in its community.

*Dining room*

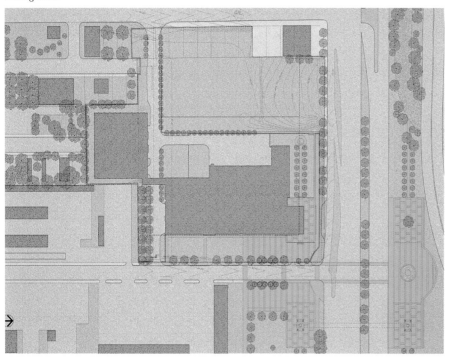

*Site plan*

0    80    160 ft

*View from Gillette Street and Allen Parkway*

*View from Allen Parkway looking toward downtown Houston*

# Discovery Square Master Plan

*Erie, Pennsylvania, 2000*

The program for the Concept Master Plan for Discovery Square includes new galleries, support space and classrooms for the Erie Art Museum, new exhibit space and classrooms for the Children's Museum, and shared facilities such as a common lobby, enclosed courtyard and sculpture garden, orientation center, gift shop, café, collection storage areas, workshops and offices.

The master plan takes advantage of and reinforces the existing mixed-use nature of the area by retaining the three existing museum buildings and their individual identities when viewed from State and French Streets. The primary public access to Discovery Square is located on Fifth Street with a secondary pedestrian door on Fourth. These entrances, at approximately mid-block, are linked by a three-story spine — an interior street — that establishes a clear literal and figurative link among the three institutions and provides access to the central atrium and various common program spaces. The proposed materials and articulation are meant to tie Discovery Square to its context without specific stylistic reference.

*View from Fifth and French Streets*

*Fifth Street elevation*

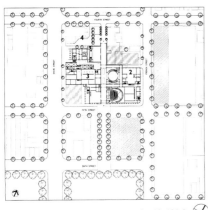

1 Theater
2 Children's Museum
3 History museum
4 Erie Art Museum

*Site and ground floor plan*     0  60  120 ft

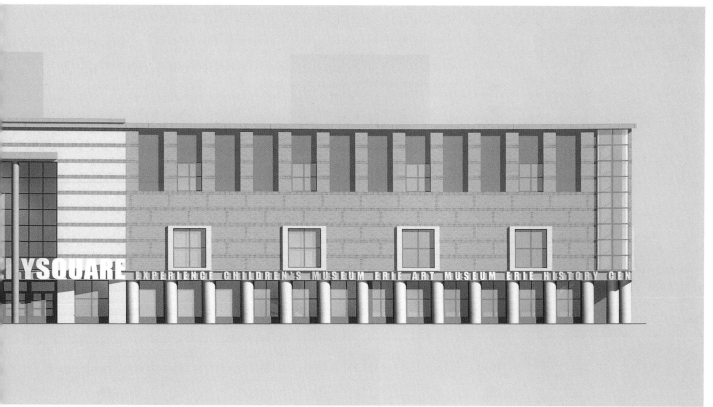

# United States Embassy Compound

*Seoul, Korea, 2000*

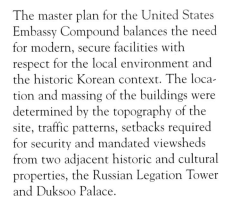

The master plan for the United States Embassy Compound balances the need for modern, secure facilities with respect for the local environment and the historic Korean context. The location and massing of the buildings were determined by the topography of the site, traffic patterns, setbacks required for security and mandated viewsheds from two adjacent historic and cultural properties, the Russian Legation Tower and Duksoo Palace.

The first phase replaces out-of-date housing with an eight-story apartment building for diplomatic families. The buildings are compatible in scale with other mid-rise buildings adjacent to the site. The second phase involves construction of the chancery office building on the northern, flatter portion of the site. At 15 stories, the chancery fits within the context of tall modern commercial buildings at north edge of the site.

The entire site inside the walls of the compound is developed as a series of landscaped gardens. A large lawn provides common open space to resident families. Other more intimate picturesque spaces are reminiscent of traditional Korean gardens, acknowledging the local reverence for natural landscape.

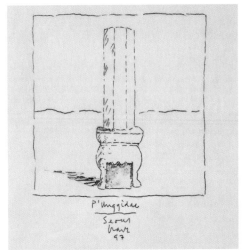

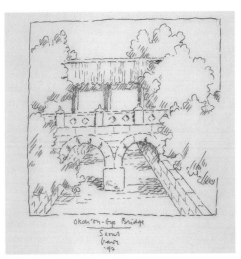

*Referential sketches*

*Chancery office building view from the garden*

*Housing view from the garden*

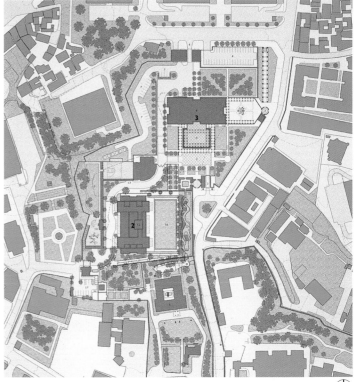

1 Existing ambassador's
  residence
2 Housing
3 Chancery office
  building

*Site plan*

0  15  30 m

*Master plan model*

## Mahler 4

*Amsterdam, Netherlands, 2000*

*Lobby*

Mahler 4 is a mixed-use development on the Mahlerstrasse in Amsterdam. Nine different architects were asked to design buildings to be sited above a common 2,000-car parking garage. This project is an 110,000-square-foot speculative retail and office building with a predetermined wedge-shaped footprint.

The character and detailing of the building are reminiscent of the geometric interests found in Dutch architecture of the 1920s. The ground floor, double height to accommodate the retail portion of the program, is clad in red honed marble. The six office floors above are clad in a buff-colored attenuated brick known as "Dudok" brick after the Dutch architect. At the top of the two vertical facade elements flanking the entrance courtyard, copper-barrel-vaulted roofs create special spaces on the uppermost floor to be used for conference rooms or boardrooms.

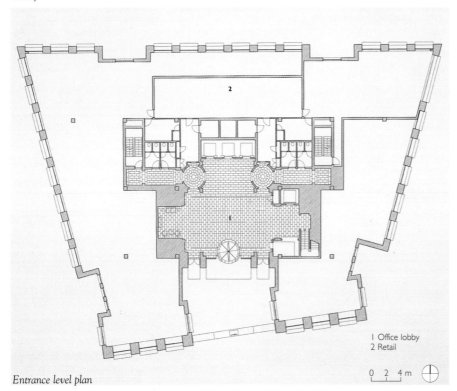

1 Office lobby
2 Retail

0 2 4 m

*Entrance level plan*

*View toward building entrance*

## Competition for the West Palm Beach Library

*West Palm Beach, Florida, 2001*

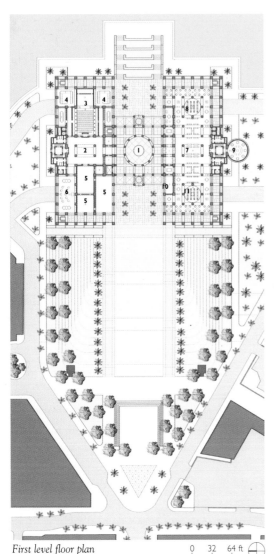

*Upper library floor plan*

*First level floor plan*

0    32    64 ft

1 Lobby
2 Community Center
   reception hall
3 Auditorium
4 Meeting room
5 Gallery
6 Art studio
7 Adult Library new
   collections display
8 Adult popular fiction
9 Café
10 Library store
11 Adult popular non-fiction

This competition entry, which was not premiated, sites the new library along the intercoastal waterway at the terminus of Clematis Street, historically the main street of West Palm Beach. Surrounding the library are plazas, pergolas, an outdoor amphitheater and steps leading down to the water; all of which enhance public use of the site.

The first level of the library contains the main lobby, circulation desk and community spaces such as a café, auditorium, galleries, art studios, library store and bookstore, built above an on-grade service level. The mezzanine contains staff offices and workrooms, the genealogy collection and the seniors' area. The Children's Library and Multimedia Area occupy the second level, and the Adult Library is located at the top of the building.

The lower levels of the library have extensive windows that provide a transparent quality and allow views through the building to the water from upper Clematis Street. A dramatic frame in the form of a truncated cone rises in the center of the building, creating an iconic landmark on the water.

*Model view from the water*

*Section*

# Dameisha Resort
# Master Plan

*Shenzhen, China, 2001*

The master plan for this 260-room resort hotel in Shenzhen, China emphasizes the relationship between architecture and the natural landscape. The hotel is organized as a series of buildings sited along the beach and oriented toward the water. The main building surrounds an informal courtyard with various food and beverage functions.

Two seven-story buildings house the majority of guestrooms. Suites are located in the wings with presidential suites located in circular elements closest to the water. Additional guestrooms are provided in villas sited along the beach. This organizational strategy provides a sense of community at a domestic scale while preserving the privacy of individual quarters. The teahouse at the eastern end of the site is a quiet place reminiscent of Chinese traditions.

Throughout the resort, the buildings are given a distinctive identity through a playful architectural character that integrates the openness of a resort hotel with site-specific concerns to connect the development to the city and an adjacent park. Extensive landscaping with indigenous tropical vegetation provides shade and complements the buildings.

*Aerial view of the resort*

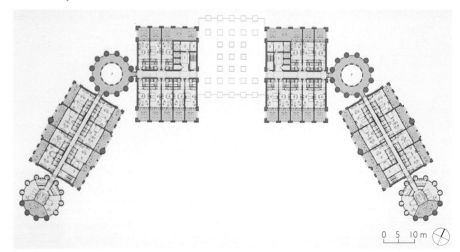

0  5  10 m

*Main hotel building plan*

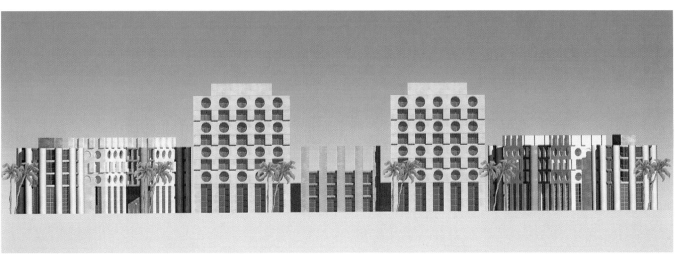

*Main hotel building elevation*

Guestroom group elevation

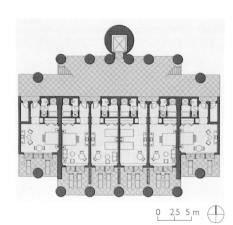

Guestroom group plan

Guestroom group elevation

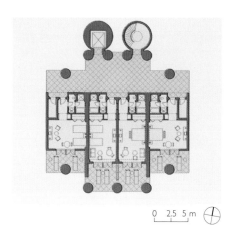

Guestroom group plan

284

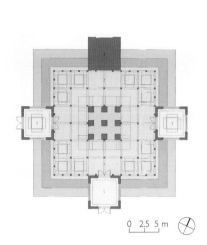

Teahouse plan

Teahouse elevation

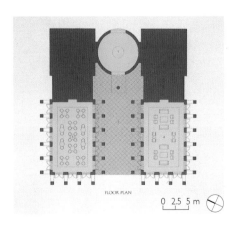

Marina restaurant pavilion plan

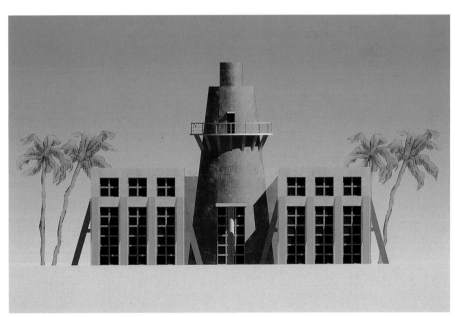

Marina restaurant pavilion elevation

## Competition for the
## United States Institute of Peace
*Washington, D.C., 2001*

The United States Institute of Peace, which sponsors exhibitions, education and conference functions, is sited on Constitution Avenue facing the Mall. An elliptical Peace Garden creates a forecourt and reconciles the symmetrical organization of the building with the triangular configuration of the site. The ellipse, which is also expressed in the glass dome above the entrance pavilion, embodies formal principles that contribute to the symbolism of the institution. As described by Thomas Jefferson, pre-eminent American President and architect, the ellipse is characterized by two centers that create one pure geometric form—in essence two entities resolved in a perfect whole—a paradigm for negotiating peace.

Central to the composition is a domed cylindrical pavilion containing the entrance lobby on the ground floor and a Great Hall for special events on the second floor. The glass dome, glistening by day and radiating at night, creates a recognizable and symbolic image for the institution. This scheme was not chosen for further development.

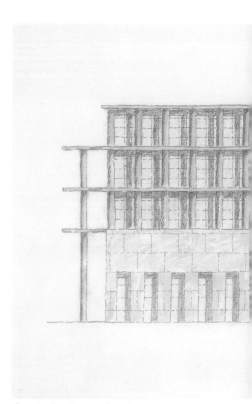

*Constitution Avenue elevation*

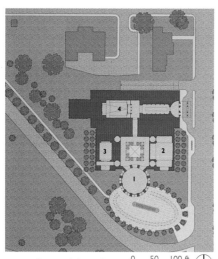

1 Lobby/exhibition
2 Exhibition
3 Multipurpose room
4 Auditorium

*Site and ground floor plan*    0    50    100 ft

*View from Constitution Avenue*

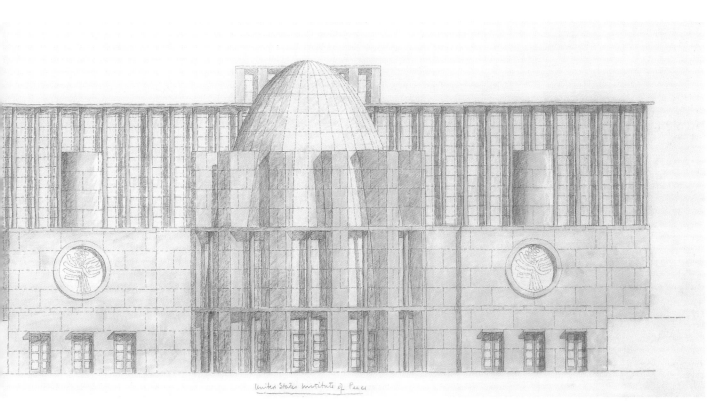

United States Institute of Peace

287

Minneapolis Institute of Arts

*Minneapolis, Minnesota, 2001*

*Atrium lobby*

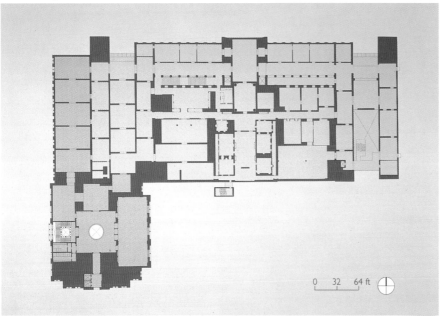

0   32   64 ft

*Gallery floor plan*

The Minneapolis Institute of Arts occupies a 1915 neoclassical building designed by McKim, Mead & White, to which two modern wings by Kenzo Tange were added in the 1970s. The four-story, 117,000-square-foot museum expansion is organized in two sections facing Stevens Street. A linear addition is located in front of the Tange wing, and a square block is located to the south. The ground floor contains public study rooms for the library and collections of works on paper and a small gallery organized around a central skylit atrium. The top floor houses a reception hall and prefunction space. The intermediate levels contain galleries connected to renovated space in the existing building.

The design of the new facades addresses both the neoclassical character of the original building and the abstract modernism of the 1970s additions. Like the McKim, Mead & White building, the composition of the expansion uses rhythm, symmetry and surface relief to articulate the facades and make the architectural language accessible. Like the Tange additions, the surfaces are simple and unadorned. The light, monochromatic masonry materials are similar to both and help unify the appearance of the complex.

*Preliminary garden elevation*

*Preliminary Stevens Street elevation*

*Stevens Street elevation*

Children's Theatre Company

*Minneapolis, Minnesota, 2001*

IMPRESSIONISM
JAN 15 - MAR 31

ANCIENT CITIES
APR 15 - JUN 30

ASIAN ART IN THE
20TH CENTURY
JUL 15 - SEP 30

THE NEW YORK FIVE
DEC 31

FORD FREE

FORD FREE

MIA CTC

*New theatre*

The Children's Theatre Company occupies one of the wings designed by Kenzo Tange and added to the Minneapolis Institute of Arts in the 1970s. The program for the 45,000-square-foot expansion includes a 290-seat flexible theatre, rehearsal space, and educational facilities, as well as renovation of the existing 720-seat theatre and backstage areas. A new theatre lobby is planned adjacent to the Third Street entrance shared with the MIA. The lobby, a dramatic multistory space with glass walls and a glass dome, assumes a luminous presence at the terminus of the Avenue of the Arts where it both enlivens the pedestrian level of the street and creates an iconic presence for the arts campus.

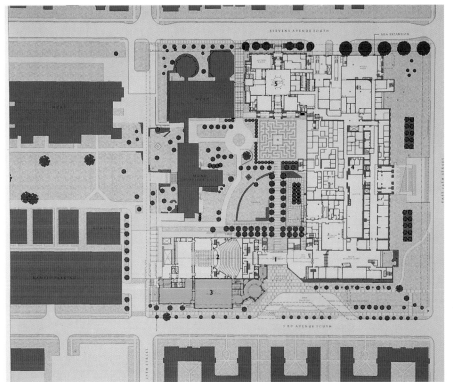

*Site and ground floor plan of the MIA and CTC*

0    64    128 ft

1 Shared MIA/CTC lobby
2 Existing CTC
3 CTC expansion
4 Existing MIA
5 MIA expansion

*Atrium lobby*

# Study for St. Charles Porte d'Aix

*Marseilles, France, 2001*

*View from the west*

This potential mixed-use project is located on a prominent site in the district known as St. Charles Porte d'Aix near the Arc de Triomphe in the Place Jules Guesde. A three-star hotel located in the center of the building holds the streetwall along Boulevard Charles Nedelec and creates a crescent-shaped public plaza for automobile drop-off along Boulevard Du Bois.

The hotel is flanked by retail stores on the ground floor and commercial office space above. These three functional sections are separated by arched openings on the ground floor, which provide pedestrian circulation through the building. The western end of the building culminates in a monumental rotunda that offers premier office and retail space and acknowledges the nearby Arc de Triomphe with the details of its design.

The massing and character of the building correspond with the prevailing architecture in this section of Marseilles. Its materials and detailing, including the tile roofs, exterior shutters, decorative metal railings and roof terraces, reflect building traditions in the region of the Mediterranean.

*Model view facing Boulevard Du Bois*

*Site and ground floor plan*

0  5  10 m

## Three on the Bund

*Shanghai, China, 2001*

Following a meticulous exterior restoration of the seven-story landmark Beaux-Arts building known as Three on the Bund, the interior, which was dramatically altered over the years, is transformed into a modern, vibrant art and retail center. The lower three floors contain fashion retail stores and art galleries. The upper floors contain upscale restaurants for notable international chefs. A seventh-floor cafe and jazz club opens onto a landscaped roof terrace.

The renovation creates an open, public image by reorganizing internal circulation and introducing a central Grand Stair. The walls surrounding the skylit Grand Stair are clad in translucent alabaster, creating a diaphanous shaft of light through the building. Two full-height atria provide vertical orientation and allow daylight to penetrate to all floors. The east atrium, with its inwardly tilting walls and round columns backed by piers of richly figured green marble, is reminiscent of a mountain forest. In contrast, the quieter west atrium is clad in red stone and penetrated with circular windows into the private dining rooms of the restaurant levels.

*East atrium*

*East atrium*

*Three on the Bund*

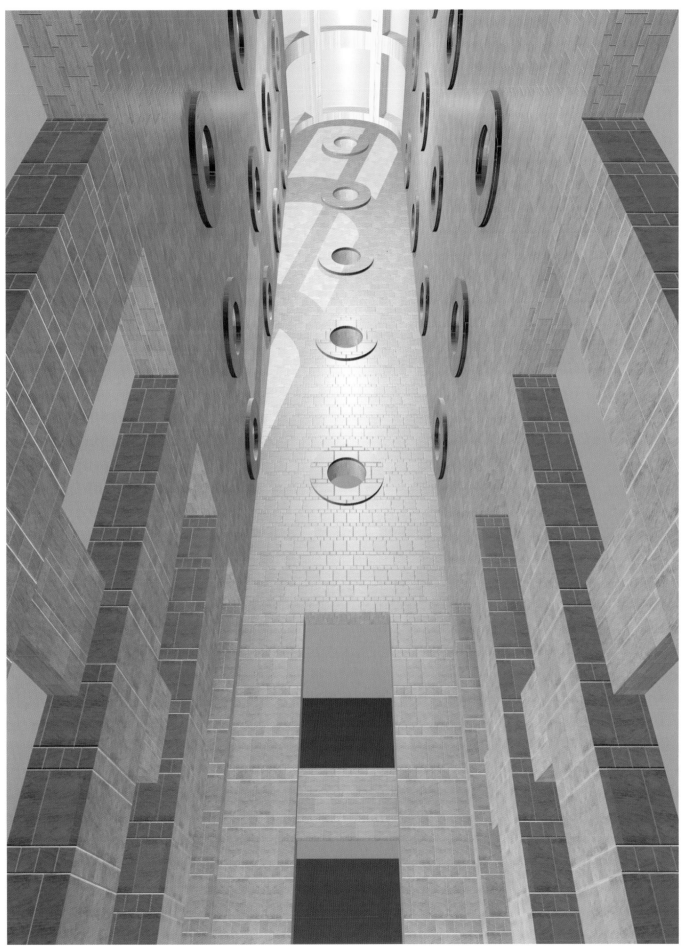

*West atrium*

*Preliminary view of a bar*

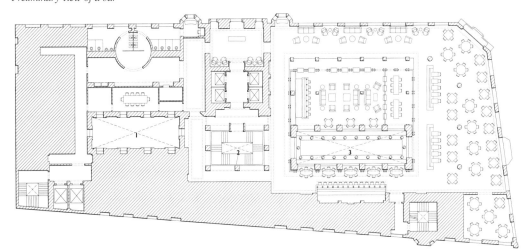

*Typical restaurant level plan*

1 West atrium
2 Grand stair
3 East atrium

0  2.5  5 m

*Preliminary view of a dining room*

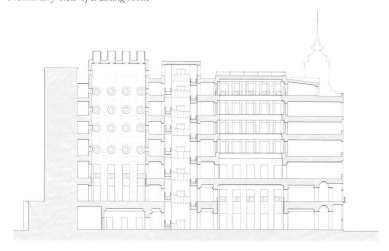

*Section through west atrium, grand stair and east atrium*

0  5  10 m

# House at Sagaponac

*Southampton, New York, 2001*

The Houses at Sagaponac, located in Southampton on Long Island, New York, is a unique development community of contemporary houses designed by 34 prominent international architects. The houses are all designed to create environmentally conscious single-family dwellings ranging in size from 2,000 to 4,500 square feet. They are intended to be modest without compromising artistic vision.

The Sagaponac house designed by Michael Graves & Associates is a retreat for weekends and vacations. The program includes a living room, dining room, library, kitchen and two bedrooms in the main house, with options for a studio and a garage flanking the house on either side. These three components form a central courtyard that creates a sense of arrival and also provides privacy for the house. The rear yard, with its sunken amphitheater, echoes the privacy of the front court. A circle of trees encloses this space, creating the feeling of an outdoor room. A small folly, perhaps a pool house or a gazebo, marks the end of the primary axis.

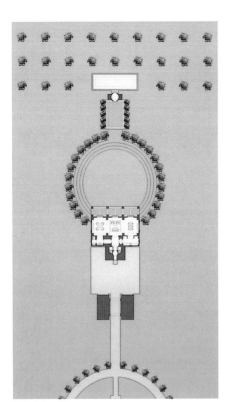

*Site plan*

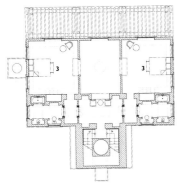

*Second floor plan*

1 Living/dining
2 Kitchen
3 Bedroom

0  4  8 ft

*Ground Floor Plan*

*Entrance elevation*

*Garden elevation*

# St. Coletta's School

*Washington, D.C., 2002*

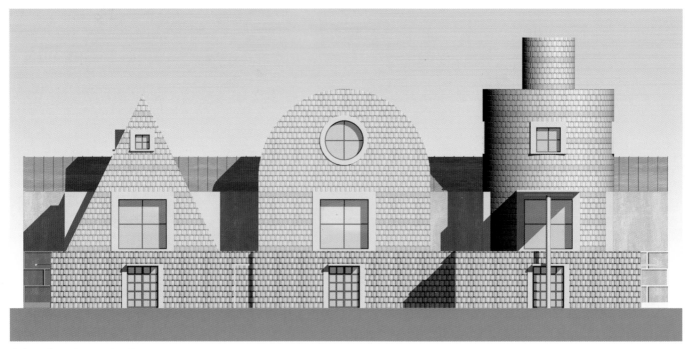

*Independence Avenue elevation*

The new campus for St. Coletta's School, nationally recognized for excellence in special education, is located in the Southeast District of Washington D.C. at the corner of Independence and 19th Street, near the Stadium-Armory Metro station. The site is also adjacent to a residential neighborhood of single-family homes. Three tile-clad multistory pavilions establish the school's identity on Independence and contain the primary public spaces, including a multipurpose room to be shared with the community.

The classrooms, designated as "houses," are designed with a scale and organization similar to the residential neighborhood along 19th Street, including those immediately across the street. The building is substantially set back from the sidewalk, which accommo-dates the Metro's right-of-way and creates a landscaped area for outdoor instruction. Each classroom "house" corresponds to a different age group and contains divisible instructional space, offices, tutoring rooms, bathrooms and an elevator. A central three-story skylit hall, called the "Village Green" organizes the scheme along a single axis. The gymnasium, available to the community, is located in an adjacent structure connected to the school.

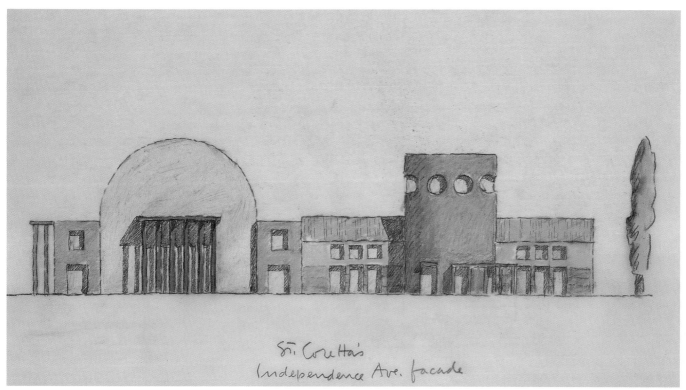

*Preliminary Independence Avenue elevation*

*Preliminary 19th Street elevation*

INDEPENDENCE AVENUE S.E.

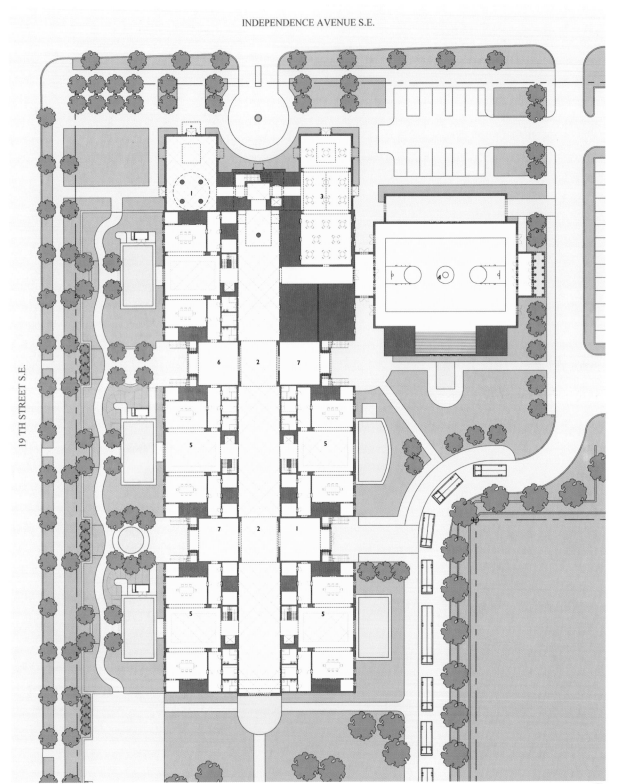

19 TH STREET S.E.

*Site and ground floor plan*

1 Lobby
2 "Village Green"
3 Community room
4 Gymnasium
5 Classroom "houses"
6 Music studio
7 Health services

0    20    40 ft

*Model view from Independence Avenue and 19th Street*

*Model view from Independence Avenue*

# Department of Transportation Headquarters

*Washington, D.C., 2002*

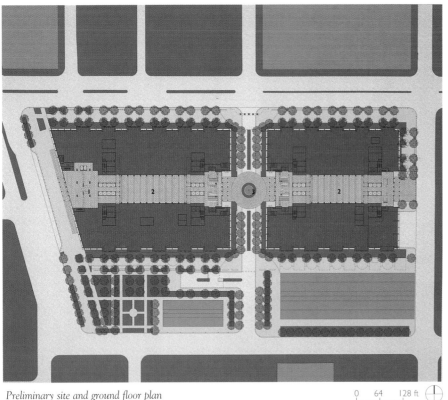

*Preliminary site and ground floor plan*

0    64    128 ft

1 New Jersey Avenue
   entrance
2 Atrium
3 Third Street

The headquarters of the United States Department of Transportation is sited in the Southeast Federal Center between federal and commercial Washington, adjacent to the Navy Yard Historic District and the Anacostia River waterfront. Spanning two full city blocks, the 1.35-million-square-foot project is developed as two separate but architecturally similar office buildings above a common below-grade parking garage.

Both buildings relate in character to the prevailing industrial context. The western building is nine stories high, while the eastern building occupies eight stories. The difference in height creates variety along M Street and emphasizes the primacy of the western building and its public entrance along New Jersey Avenue, a L'Enfant Plan boulevard within view of the Capitol Building. The New Jersey Avenue facade has a presence appropriate to the importance of a cabinet-level federal institution. The entrance portico and multistory lobby lead to adjacent first-floor space containing large departmental assembly and joint-use facilities. A central linear atrium is developed in each of the buildings. While the buildings are not physically connected across Third Street, the transparency of each building's atrium helps create a visual link between them.

*Preliminary view from New Jersey Avenue*

# New Jersey State Police Headquarters Master Plan

*West Trenton, New Jersey, 2002*

*Aerial view from the south*

The master plan for the headquarters and training center for the New Jersey State Police creates a campus that integrates new construction with existing buildings and preserves the natural landscape. Several plateaus are established within the hilly terrain to accommodate new buildings and large-scale outdoor functions requiring flat sites, such as the parade ground, running track and driver training area.

The various functional components of the program are organized hierarchically from the most publicly accessible and visible activities to those requiring a greater level of privacy and security. Each functional group is organized around a formal open space, promoting a sense of common purpose and camaraderie. Although the buildings have individual identities

appropriate to their uses, the similarities of organization and consistent use of brick and wood materials create a unified campus.

The state-of-the-art training center comprises the Police Academy's administrative headquarters, dining hall, classrooms and auditorium grouped around a quadrangle to the east of the campus entrance. The headquarters complex, consisting of a 200,000-square-foot office building, two dormitories and a fitness center surround a tree-lined parade ground, the most significant ceremonial space within the campus.

1 Existing museum
2 Dining
3 Police Academy Training Center
4 Headquarters office building
5 Parade ground
6 Dormitories
7 Fitness center
8 Driver training

*Site Plan*

0  100  200 ft

# Competition for the Jacksonville Library

*Jacksonville, Florida, 2002*

*Monroe Street elevatiom*

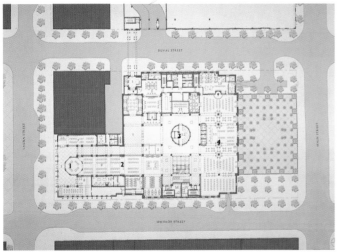

*Ground Floor Plan*

1 Entrance
2 Popular library
3 Theater
4 Children's library

0    32    64 ft

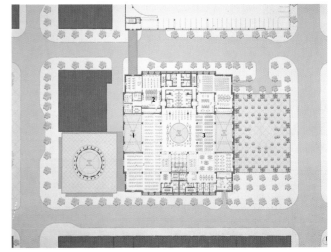

*Third level mezzanine plan*

1 Adult collection
2 Adult learning center
3 Young adult collection

The library is organized as two simple, legible volumes, a three-story entrance pavilion facing Hemming Plaza adjacent to the existing MOMA building, and a six-story building occupying the center of the site. The facades are proportioned to give the library a civic presence and yet, with its generous fenestration and sun control devices, the building is given a sense of openness appropriate for a public educational institution. As required by the program, the public spaces throughout the building are completely open. Vertical circulation among floors via escalators and glass elevators encourage the visual experience of the library's offerings. Positioning separate service cores for patrons and staff at the building's perimeter maintains the sense of transparency throughout the center of the building.

*Lobby*

# Resort Master Plan

*Canary Islands, 2002*

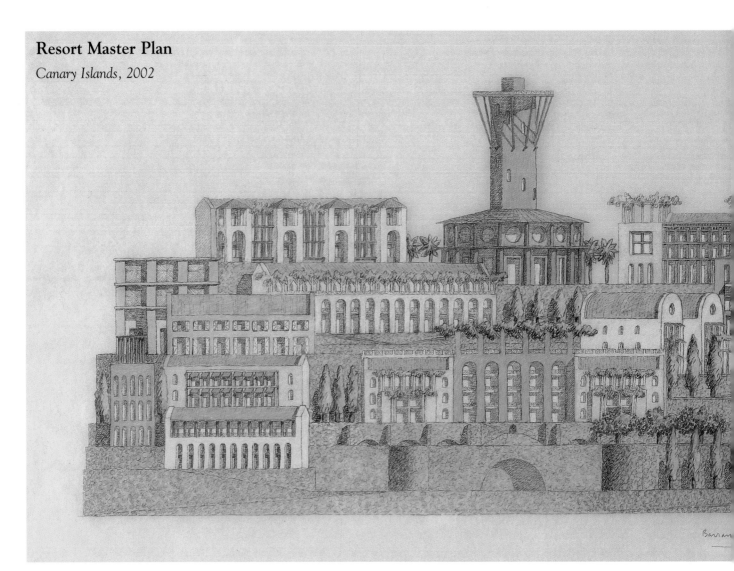

*Hilltown elevation*

*Beachfront*

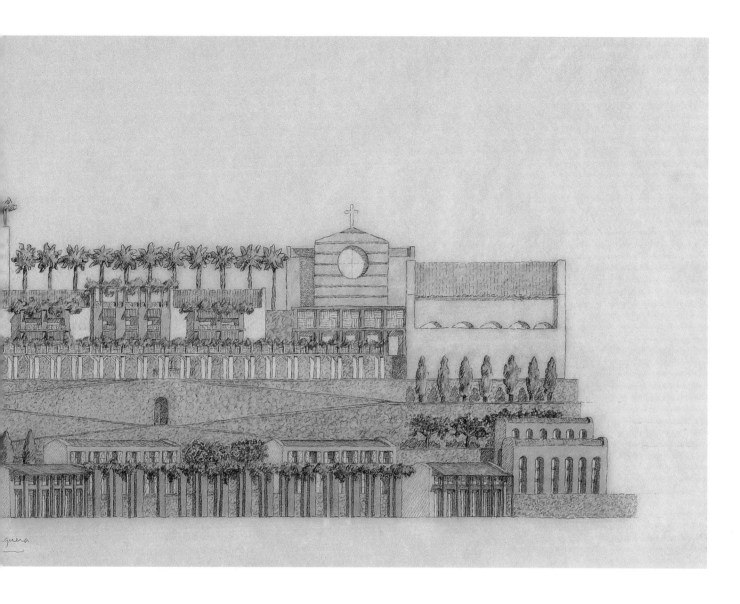

The master plan for a resort in the Canary Islands combines exciting recreational experiences with a sensible approach to land use and environmental issues. The character of the resort is inspired by the valley landscape and embraces traditional architecture of the region. One of the planning goals is to preserve the natural landscape and concentrate development to minimize disruption of the terrain. Therefore, instead of developing tennis courts, swimming pools and other recreational facilities requiring flat land throughout the resort, those facilities are concentrated in a Town Center sited on the naturally level terrain adjacent to the waterfront. An expanded beach with clubs, retail and cafes, a pier for ocean expeditions and a marina maximize opportunities for waterfront recreation. Golf courses following the contours of the valley floor

and lower ridges are selectively planted and irrigated with recycled gray water.

Various types of guest accommodations are provided in terraced hotels overlooking the ocean or the golf course, in upper levels of Town Center buildings and in hilltowns. In reaction to the proliferation of generic hotels with no ties to local context, the hilltowns are imbued with an architectural character particular to the terrain, climate and the building traditions of the region. Organizing the buildings in small-scale increments responsive to the topography creates a wide variety of courtyards, gardens and piazzas, which are lively and active in the public realm and intimate and peaceful in the private guest quarters.

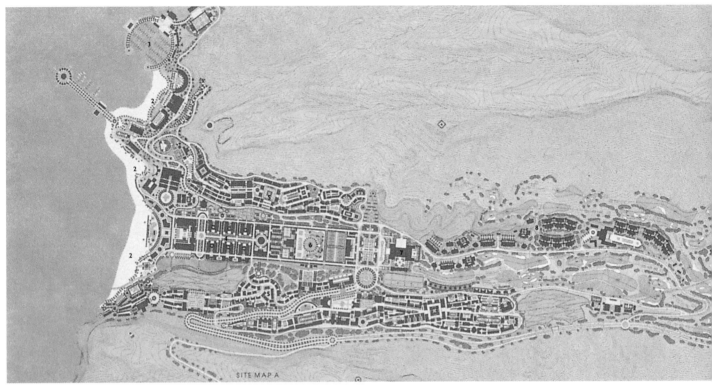

*Site plan*

1 Beach club
2 Beach hotels
3 Marina
4 Town Center
5 Hilltown
6 Swimming/tennis centers
7 Conference center
8 Golf hotel
9 Golf club
10 Equestrian center

*Alternative Town Center site plan*

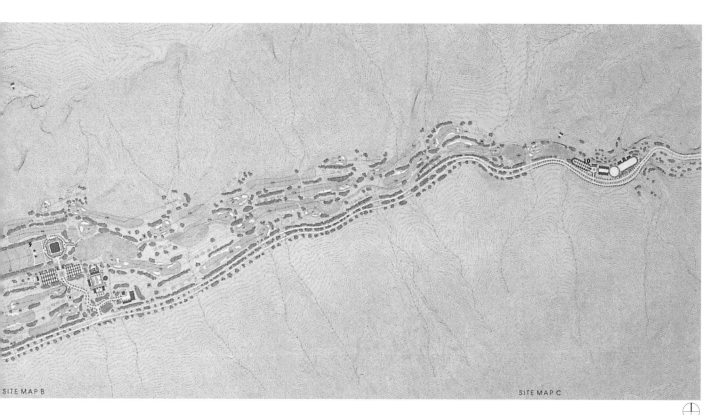

SITE MAP B

SITE MAP C

*Resort entrance and equestrian center*

*Golf clubhouse*

321

*Town Center elevation*

*Beach club elevation*

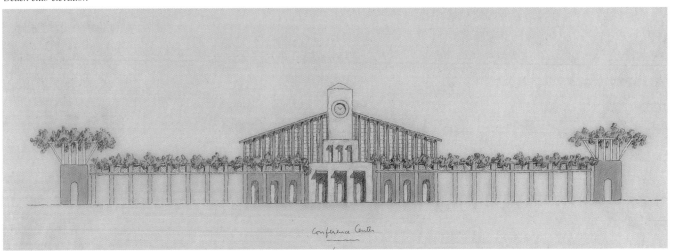

*Conference center elevation*

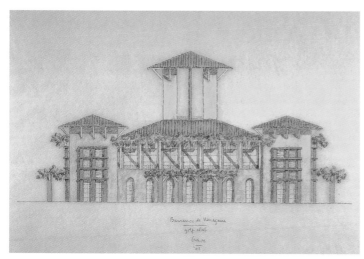

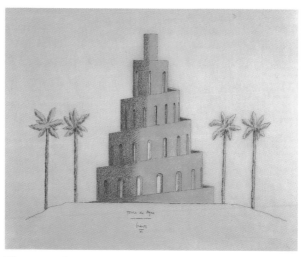

Golf clubhouse elevation

Water tower elevation

Town Center

Town Center

*Beach club*

*Town Center*

# Kennedy Center
# Expansion Study

*Washington, D.C., 2002*

*View of civic plaza and exhibitions pavilion from the Kennedy Center*

The expansion of the John F. Kennedy Center for the Performing Arts reconnects the institution to Washington's monumental core by building a deck over the adjacent highway and constructing a pair of buildings on top. In addition to providing much-needed program space, the project creates an opportunity to reaffirm the center as a living memorial to President Kennedy through the character of the new civic plaza and its architecture.

In both of the formal plan options the expansion consists of two buildings embracing a dramatic public space centered on the Kennedy Center. One of the buildings contains a café and gift shop, exhibits and educational facilities, and administrative offices. Its companion building contains restaurants on the plaza level and

rehearsal space and offices on other levels. A pair of flanking towers, which create a gate to the new plaza, accentuates the axis of E Street, the major connection to the city. Aligned with the existing Hall of States and Hall of Nations, the towers also frame the view toward Washington from inside the Kennedy Center. The civic plaza is developed as an urban garden for the arts, grand in scale but intimate in character. Two pavilions — one for exhibitions and the other for performances — pull some of the most visible activities of the program out into the public realm and, through their iconic forms, enhance the dramatic character of the place.

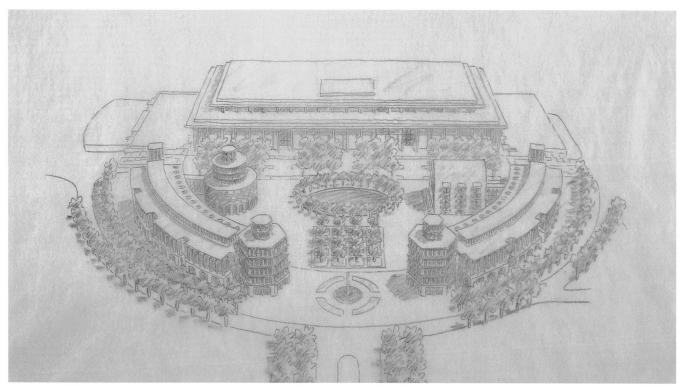

*Aerial view of Option 1 from E Street*

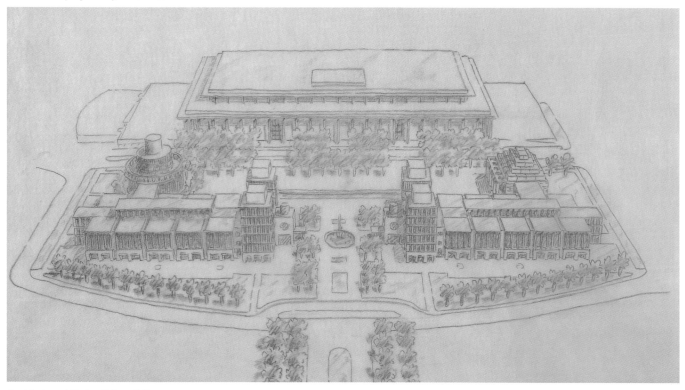

*Aerial view of Option 2 from E Street*

327

## South Campus Master Plan
## Rice University

*Houston, Texas, 2002*

This master plan studies the south and west portions of the Rice University campus, including the adjacent Main Street and University Boulevard, and assesses the impact of new development on the existing academic campus. It also considers urban relationships between the nearby Texas Medical Center and the university while addressing mass transportation, parking and automobile and pedestrian circulation in relation to both the campus and the surrounding neighborhoods.

A space utilization study for the entire campus of academic, administrative and residential components formed the basis for the physical master plan. This work included a more detailed program study for the School of Natural Science, the School of Engineering and the Athletics Department as well as for student recreation, arts-related programs and retail space. Major components of the master plan program comprise a 3,500-seat convocation center, student centers, four future residential colleges, research and academic facilities. The study follows the original Cram-Goodhue master plan by increasing the density of the existing campus through adding rooms to existing residential colleges and adding new residential colleges to existing residential quadrangles. The major and minor axes of the original master plan are extended as a new quadrangle is planned to the south, terminated with a new entrance to the campus opposite the Texas Medical Center on Main Street and reinforced by landscaping with the live oaks typical on the campus. Proposed long-term expansion of the campus is meant to extend the original plan strategies to new quadrangles similar in scale to those existing but which can also accommodate the more flexible floor plates needed in modern academic research buildings.

*Site plan*

MASTER PLAN
SCHEME A
RICE UNIVERSITY
HOUSTON, TEXAS

PATHS
FIELDS
STRUCTURED PARKING
EXISTING BUILDINGS
NEW BUILDINGS

NEW BUILDINGS:
1.  CONVOCATION/RECREATION
2.  NEW RESIDENTIAL COLLEGE
3.  ACADEMIC EXPANSION
4.  PERFORMING ARTS
5.  SATELLITE CENTRAL PLANT
6.  HOUSING
7.  STUDENT CENTER
8.  STRUCTURED PARKING
9.  VARSITY TENNIS

DECEMBER 10, 2002
MICHAEL GRAVES & ASSOCIATES

## Arts and Sciences Building
## New Jersey City University

*Jersey City, New Jersey, 2002*

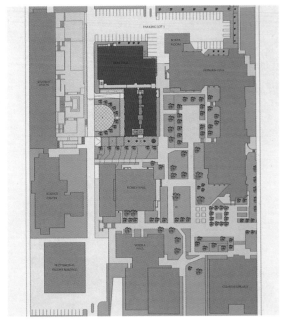

Site plan

0  30  60 ft

The Arts and Sciences Building largely replaces Fries Hall, an existing building on the site, and comprises six stories plus a lower level that opens to grade as the site slopes down to the west. The building program provides offices and teaching space for several departments, including 14 new classrooms and 10 computer laboratories.

The building's massing reflects its pivotal location on the campus. A two-story exterior colonnade along the south facade responds to major circulation paths connecting Hepburn Hall, the historic heart and symbol of the university, to the much-frequented Student Union. A distinctive entrance tower at the southeast corner of the building creates a new visual focal point for this section of the campus. The Dean's conference room is located on the upper floor of the tower beneath a pyramidal roof.

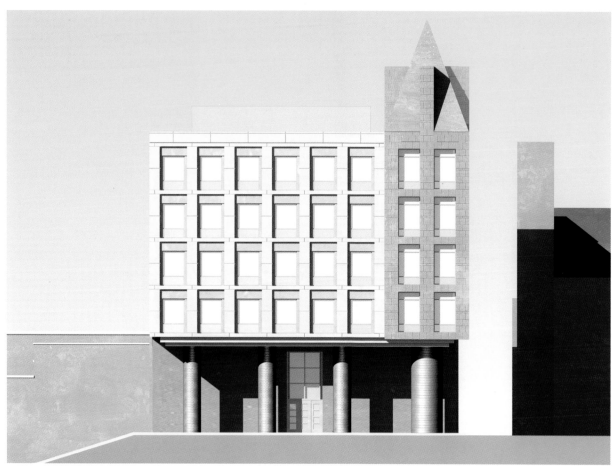

West elevation

South elevation

## Expansion of the Kavli Institute for Theoretical Physics

## University of California at Santa Barbara

*Santa Barbara, California, 2002*

1 Auditorium
2 Enclosed courtyard
3 New office wing
4 Existing building

*Site and ground floor plan*

*Enclosed courtyard*

The 11,500-square-foot expansion of the Institute for Theoretical Physics, designed by Michael Graves & Associates and completed in 1994, provides additional offices and meeting rooms, and a new 50-seat auditorium for a variety of conferences and presentations. The plan of the original building features two wings in a V-shaped configuration with a courtyard in the center. The expansion connects the two wings and fills in the western end of the courtyard with a first floor auditorium and second floor offices. The remaining area of the courtyard, now covered with a steel and glass roof canopy, becomes a prefunction space. The composition, character, colors and materials of the expansion are in keeping with the picturesque and informal nature of the original building.

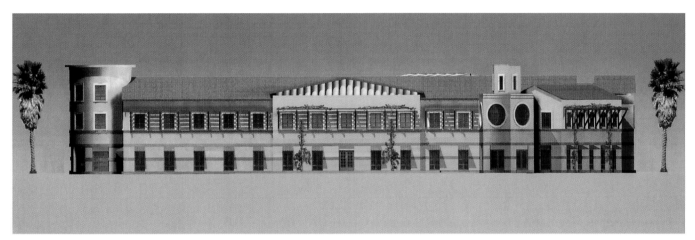

*South elevation*

*East elevation*

*View from the south lawn*

# Kasteel Holterveste

*Den Bosch, Netherlands, 2003*

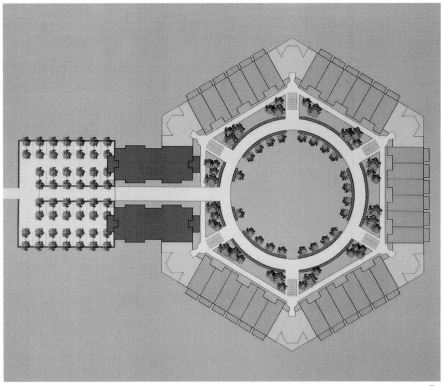

Site and ground floor plan

0 5 10 m

Aerial view of the development

Kasteel Holterveste is the sixth of nine multifamily residential projects in Haverleij, a large development located in Den Bosch near Eindhoven. The program consists of 68 dwellings, including 48 single-family houses and 20 apartments, plus parking. Consistent with Haverleij's master plan, each development is characterized as a castle, the Dutch word for which is "kasteel." Kasteel Holterveste is organized as a hexagon. Five sides feature three-story houses, and the sixth side is designed as a gate flanked by apartment buildings and leading to the interior garden court. Four house towers with peaked roofs articulate the intersections of the sides of the hexagon and serve as iconic markers creating the image of Kasteel Holterveste as seen from the landscape of the surrounding golf course.

The architectural character is inspired by the Amsterdam School architectural movement of the 1920s, which featured a modern and somewhat abstract use of brick without sacrificing the scale and detail that provide a sense of domesticity.

*Courtyard facade detail*

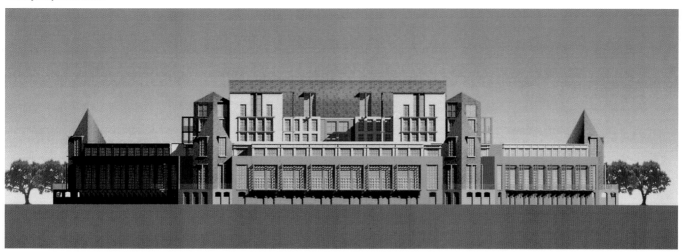

*Rear elevation*

# Club Wedd House

*2003*

*View of the entrance*

Target Stores commissioned a house as the first prize in a sweepstakes for couples listed in the store's bridal registry. The house is designed to be flexible in the use of the rooms, the options for exterior materials and colors, and future expansion. The plan is organized symmetrically about the central entrance and a two-story living room. The house is designed as a kit home to be fabricated by Lindal Cedar Homes of Seattle, Washington. Its architectural character is derived from the wooden post and beam construction system and expressed through the timber frame detailing and wood siding.

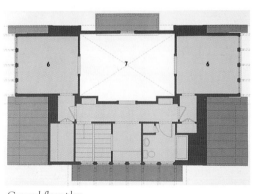

*Ground floor plan*

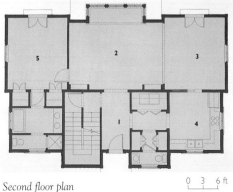

*Second floor plan*

1. Foyer
2 Living room
3 Dining room
4 Kitchen
5 Master bedroom
6 Bedroom
7 Open to below

0   3   6 ft

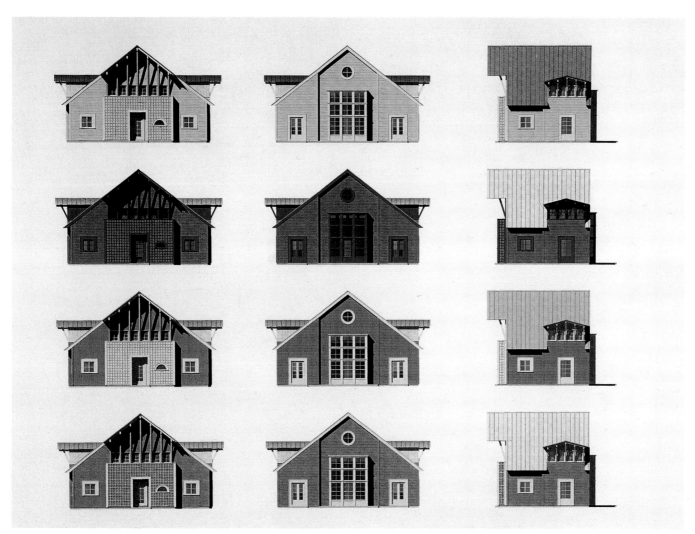

*Facade siding and color options*

# Pavilions™

## 2003

The Pavilions™ continue a tradition of outbuildings as architectural accessories for the home. Customarily, a pavilion is an exceptional room in an estate, a whimsical complement to the residence proper. Thus it can vary in color and style from the main residence. The Pavilions™, developed in partnership with target.com and Lindal Cedar Homes of Seattle, Washington, are part of a long tradition of American kit homes shipped all over the country and assembled on site.

The impetus to design the Pavilions™ came from the desire to offer homeowners the option of adding flexible space to a house without the inconvenient disruption often associated with adding a room. A Pavilion either can be built as a freestanding structure or, using a door or window opening, can be attached to an existing house via an "extended threshold."

The Pavilions™ are available in three models with a variety of options for colors and siding design: Brighton, an octagonal pavilion useful as a breakfast room, dining room, garden room or studio; Heathcote, a square room useful as a media room, home office, game room or library; and Sherwood, an open-air or screened room ideal for a garden room or a porch.

*Brighton pavilion*

*Brighton pavilion study*

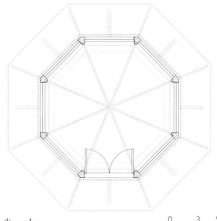

*Brighton pavilion plan*

0   3   5 ft

*Sherwood pavilion*

*Heathcote pavilion*

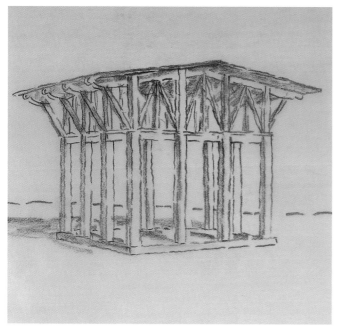

*Sherwood pavilion study*

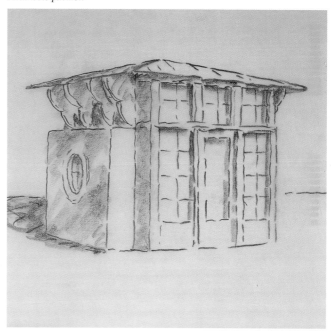

*Heathcote pavilion study*

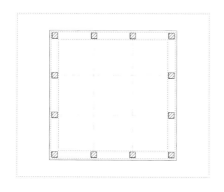

*Sherwood pavilion plan*

0   3   5 ft

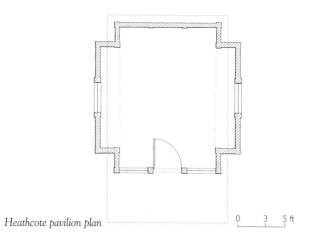

*Heathcote pavilion plan*

0   3   5 ft

# Campus Master Plan
# Florida Tech

*Melbourne, Florida, 2003*

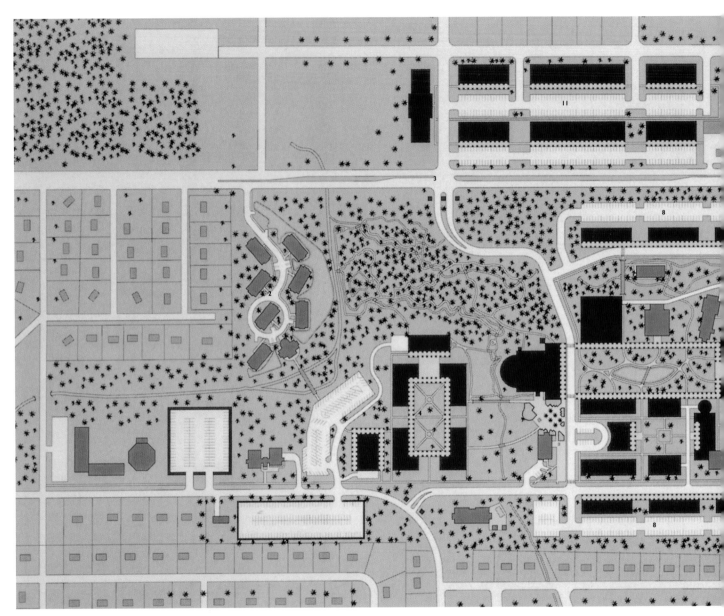

*Long-range master plan, with existing buildings in light terra cotta and new phased construction in dark red*

In order to accommodate future growth in university programs and student population, Florida Tech commissioned a master plan for its 130-acre campus that provides managed growth in four major phases over a 20-year period. The master plan proposes a hierarchical system of internal roadways and walkways that encourages the development of a coherent campus integrating academic, residential and recreational activities. The plan also proposes reinstatement of the original entrance to the campus adjacent to an extraordinary 25-acre botanical garden containing more than 200 species of palm trees. Relocating the campus entrance and developing a central quadrangle in the first phase will create a strong and immediate presence for the school. A consistent palette of exterior colors and materials for the buildings will reinforce the relationships among buildings and contribute to the campus's sense of place.

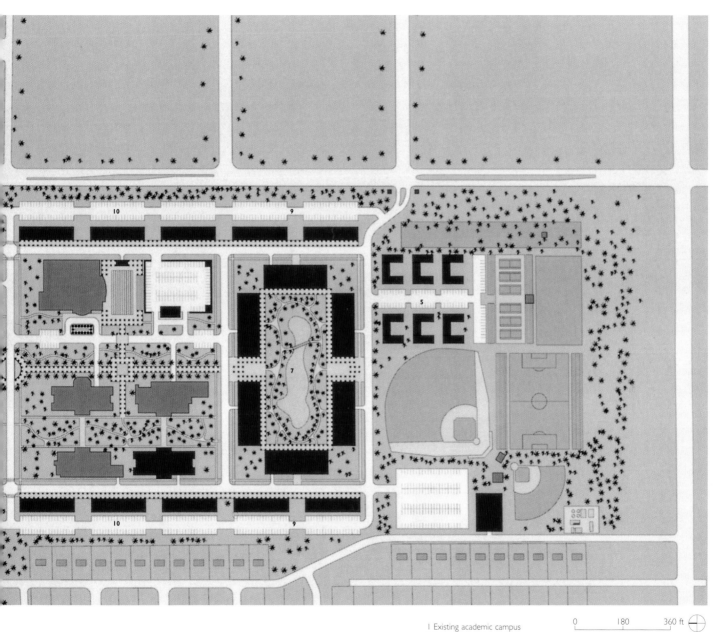

1 Existing academic campus
2 Existing student housing
3 New campus entrance
4 Phase 1 student housing
5 Phase 1 fraternity/sorority houses
6 Phase 2 academic buildings and
  dining hall, new construction and
  renovation
7 Phases 2 and 3 academic
  quadrangle
8 Phase 2 student housing
9 Phase 3 student housing
10 Phase 4 student housing
11 Phase 4 research complex and
  commercial development

0    180    360 ft

# National Automobile Museum

*The Hague, Netherlands, 2003*

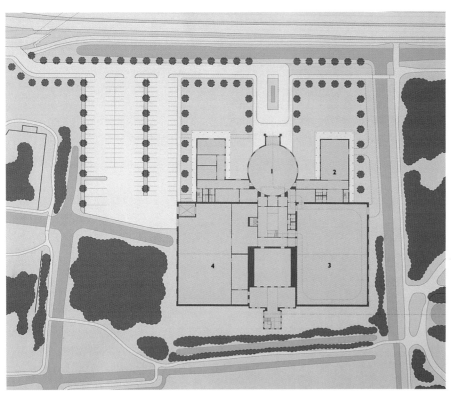

*Site and ground floor plan*

1 Entrance
2 Auditorium
3 Exhibition
4 Workshop

0   25   50 m

The National Automobile Museum is a new institution to preserve and display an extensive collection of new and vintage automobiles. It is located in a park near the Queen's residence and faces the Leidsestraatweg. Its architectural character responds to the traditional nature of the context through massing, detailing and consistent use of brick materials. In order to mitigate the large scale of the exhibit space and workshops, the smaller scale public activities are organized in a U-shaped configuration facing the street. The central rotunda, the main entrance to the museum, doubles as a temporary exhibition gallery for featured pieces. To either side, the roof overhangs and columns surrounding the auditorium and reception hall impart a domestic scale to the composition in deference to the neighborhood.

*Leidsestraatweg elevation*

*View of the entrance*

# Biographies

**Michael Graves, FAIA**

Michael Graves, FAIA, has been at the forefront of architectural design for nearly four decades. Cited by Paul Goldberger, former *New York Times* critic, as "the most truly original voice American architecture has produced in some time," Graves has influenced the transformation of urban architecture from a focus on abstract modernism to more contextual design. He has received many prestigious awards, including the 1999 National Medal of Arts and the 2001 Gold Medal from the American Institute of Architects.

A native of Indianapolis, Graves received his architectural training at the University of Cincinnati and Harvard University. In 1960, Graves received the Rome Prize and studied at the American Academy in Rome, of which he is now a Trustee. He is the Robert Schirmer Professor of Architecture, Emeritus, at Princeton University, where he taught for 39 years.

**Michael Graves & Associates**

Michael Graves founded his firm in Princeton, New Jersey in 1964. Today, Michael Graves & Associates, with offices in Princeton and in New York City, has a diversified worldwide architectural practice encompassing many building types as well as a highly successful product design practice. In addition to Graves, the principals of the firm: (in order of seniority) are: Karen Nichols, Patrick Burke, Gary Lapera, Thomas Rowe, John Diebboll and Susan Howard. The firm is organized in studios: four architecture studios, an interior design studio and several product design studios. The architecture studios are led by principals who collaborate with Michael Graves on project design.

**Karen Nichols, FAIA**

Since joining the firm in 1977, Karen Nichols, FAIA, has had overall responsibility for managing Michael Graves & Associates' practice in architecture, interior design and product design. As an architect, she has been the Principal-in-Charge of multiple phases of renovation and expansion of The Newark Museum in Newark, New Jersey, the master plan of the Detroit Institute of Arts, and the Riverbend Music Center in Cincinnati, Ohio. She received her education at Smith College and the Massachusetts Institute of Technology.

**Patrick Burke, AIA**

Principal and Studio Head, Patrick Burke, AIA, received his architectural degrees from University of Illinois, Chicago Circle and Princeton University and joined Michael Graves & Associates in 1982. Representative projects included in this monograph are: four resort hotels in Egypt; the Brussels headquarters of the international insurance company, Fortis AG; expansions of the Minneapolis Institute of Arts and the Children's Theatre Company; the Museum of the Shenandoah Valley in Virginia; and a master plan for a resort in the Canary Islands.

**Gary Lapera, AIA**

Principal and Studio Head, Gary Lapera, AIA, joined Michael Graves & Associates in 1983. Representative projects included in this monograph are: the United States Embassy Compound in Seoul, Korea; the NovaCare Complex for the Philadelphia Eagles football team; Castalia, the Ministry of Health, Welfare and Sport in The Hague; the New Jersey State Police Headquarters Master Plan; several apartment towers and mixed-use buildings in Japan; and the Pavilions and Club Wedd House. He received his education at Cornell University and Harvard University.

**Thomas P. Rowe, AIA**

Principal and Studio Head, Thomas Rowe, AIA, received his architectural education at Catholic University and Princeton University and joined Michael Graves & Associates in 1984. Representative projects included in this monograph are: the NCAA Headquarters and Hall of Champions in Indianapolis, Indiana; the headquarters of the International Finance Corporation in Washington, D.C., the O'Reilly Theater in Pittsburgh; the Houston branch of the Federal Reserve Bank of Dallas; two residential towers in New York; and several projects for Rice University in Houston.

**John Diebboll, AIA**

John Diebboll, AIA, is the Principal-in-Charge of the firm's New York studio. He was educated at Bennington College and Princeton University and joined Michael Graves & Associates in 1984. Representative projects included in this monograph are public libraries in Alexandria, Virginia and Topeka, Kansas; the Taiwan National Museum of Pre-history; the Indianapolis Art Center; 1500 Ocean Drive in Miami Beach, Florida; St. Mary's Church in Rockledge, Florida; the master plan for Florida Tech; and several private residences.

**Susan Howard**

Susan Howard has advised Michael Graves & Associates on financial and legal matters since 1987. She has played a key role in developing MGA's employment practices and business plans. She has focused her attention on diversification of the practice, in particular on the development of the interior design and product design practices. She received her undergraduate degree from Beaver College, a J.D. from Seton Hall and an L.L.M. in Taxation from New York University.

## Associated Architects and Designers

Academy-Groupe Atelier de Genval
Arcadis
Architecture & Planning Group
Atelier d'Art Urbain
Baum Associates
Buro Hoen Architecten
Burt Hill Kosar Rittelmann Architects
Crowner/King Architects
Dalton, Moran & Robinson
Daniel, Mann, Johnson & Mendenhall/Holmes & Narver
ECADI
EDAW Inc.
Rami El Dahan & Soheir Farid Architects
Grabowsky & Poort BV
HACBM
Haigo Shen & Associates
Yasuhiro Hamano
Ahmed Hamdy
Hammel Associates
HKS Inc.
Horst, Terrill & Karst, Architects
INA
Arch. Michel Jaspers & Partners
KBJ Architects
Kunwon International
Vlastimil Koubek, Architect
Maeda Construction Company, Ltd.
Massive Design Group
Min Associates
H. Thomas O'Hara, Architect
Amr Omar
Alain Poncet & Patrick Schwarz
Pierce, Goodwin, Alexander & Linville
Franco Possemato
Rafferty Rafferty and Tollefson Architects
Rolland, DelValle & Bradley
RSP Architects
Ryckaerts, Peeters and Partners
S & P Ltd.
Schmidt Associates
SERA Architects
Jose Siao Ling & Associates
SmithGroup Incorporated
STV Architects
Robert Swedroe, Architects and Planners
Tongi University
Mart van Schijndel Architect
Thomas, Miller & Partners
TSP Architects & Planners
Van den Acker Architekten
Van den Oever, Zaaijer, Roodbeen and Partners
URS Corporation
WHL-Archasia Consultants

## Project Staff

The following list represents professional and administrative staff members and professional interns employed by Michael Graves & Associates from 1995-2003. We would like to thank the numerous individuals not mentioned here who assisted our administrative staff on a short-term or part-time basis during this period.

### Principals
Michael Graves
Patrick Burke
John Diebboll
Susan Howard
Gary Lapera
Karen Nichols
Thomas Rowe

### Senior Associates & Senior Directors
Michael Crackel
William Harrington
Roisin Heneghan
Don Menke
Robert Miller
Peter Neilson
Stephen Panzarino
Pim Robberechts
Donald Strum
Edward Tuck
Gregg Wielage
Mary Yun

### Associates & Directors
J. Craig Babe
Jesse Castaneda
Adina Chouequet
Hillary Ellison
Robert Fahr
Keoni Fleming
Saverio Manago
Diana Nelson
Lyndon Neri
David Peschel
Mark Proicou
Barry Richards
Joseph Sullivan
Mark Sullivan
Joshua Zinder

### Senior Designers
Katherine Ambroziak
Heidrun Beck
Robert Blaser
Eric Bogner
Christopher Brown
Russell DiNardo
Katherine Dy
Arturo Herscovici
Antoinette Jackson
Matthew Ligas
John Orgren
Shih-fu Peng
Jil Peters
Erika Schmitt
Tony Wilson
James Wisniewski
John Wriedt

### Design Staff
Anne Adams
Sabra Albert
Brian Ambroziak
Michael Ammerman
Patricia Anahory Silva
John Anastasiadis
Kim Armour
Kristopher Artz
Emily Atwood
Giovanna Balarezo
Robert Bander
Meryl Blinder
Brian Bock
Anthony Boczkowski
Stefanie Brechbuehler
Randi Brookman
Jeffrey Brunner
David Cabianca
Antonija Campbell
Chris Campbell
Philip Chan
Grace Chen
Lin-Ann Ching
Marco Cimatti
Dorothy Colavecchio
Mark Cox
Tiffany Curtis
Lara Daniel
Jerome del Fierro
Jerome Dell'Olio
Roxanne de Prado
Elizabeth DeTeresi
Paul De Voe
Matthew Dockery
Scott Doty
Julie Dowling
Leslie Dowling
Urszula Duda
Emily Estes
Maria Fedorchenko
Elizabeth Ferrara
Justin Ferrick
Jamie Fleming
Jennifer Flume
Alex Garzon

Daniel Gatto
Danielle Gingras
George Hauner
Travis Hicks
Karen Hilde
Anthony Hron
Jiayur Hsu
Rossana Hu
Newman Huh
Earl Jackson
Brooke Johnson
Derek Jones
Joshua Jones
Esther Kardos
Tambi Kat
Michelle Kaufmann
Christine Kelley
Brook Kennedy
Christine Kennedy
Justus Kessler
Norine Kevolic
Nelson Kim
Lorissa Kimm
Xandra Kohler
David Kubik
Jason Kuhnle
Tae Wook Lah
Alan LaZare
Sangzo Lee
Hu Li
Tiffany Lin
Stephanie Magdziak
Lucy Malone
Andrew March
Karen McEvoy
Yuka Midorikawa
Coleman Mills
Shelley Miracle
Christina Noble
Kara Nykreim
Julie Nymann
Brian Pawlowski
Damon Pearson
Thomas Pen
Lisa Perrine
Richard Perry
Brendan Peters
Arturo Ponciano
Hortensia Quevedo
Raquel Raimundez
Doug Reitmeyer
Brian Revoir
Pablo Riestra

Stephanie Rigolot
Edwin Rivera
Andrew Roman
Ani Rosskam
Maria Ruiz
Kyle Ryan
Savvas Sarafidis
Annatina Schneider
Christina Seo
Stephen Skelly
Roger Smith
Jason Smith
Christopher Starkey
Dortha Starling
Shanmei Sun
Michael Sweebe
Susan Szymanski
Venina Tandela
Genie Tang
Jacqueline Teo
Teresa Thiele
Heidi Toll
Ludwing Vaca
Robert Van Varick
Kindra Welch
Irina Wong
Bonni Yelin
Ashley Yoon
Erhmei Yuan

**Senior Administrative Staff**
Deborah Baker
Kathleen P. Cherry
Nancy Festa
Caroline Hancock
Linda Kinsey
Kenneth Zauber

**Administrative Staff**
Carlos Acevedo
Dean Acquaviva
Kathryn Aptner
Karin Beauregard
Catherine Boerner
Marek Bulaj
Lisa Burke
Linda Burton-Hammell
Robert Cifelli
James Cifelli
Allison Clancy
Donna Clifton
Christina Dallas
Nicole DeCongilio

Katherine Dixon
Lisa Dockray
Elise Dodeles
Audrey Eisenstein
Andrea Ellis
Royce Epstein
Patricia Frik
Judith Gawlowski
Jennifer Geoghan
Anmei Goldsmith
Carolyn Goodridge
Adam Graves
Courtney Havran
Laura Hawkins
Janet Hickey
Holly Hyde
Janna Israel
Cara Jacobson
Eric Janson
Beatrice-Rose Johnson
Ann Johnston
Stacy Kelley
Elizabeth-Anne Kilkenny
Kathryn-Anne Kilkenny
Joel Koenigsberg
Bryan Kubik
Jason Lazarz
Payal Luthra
Eileen Mathes
Andrew Merz
Deborah Miller
Carole Nicholson
Patrick O'Leary
Kristen Palkovich
Tracy Panzarino
Ann Protinick
Christana Puzio
Emily Reeves
Suzanne Reiss
Renee Robichaud
Cary Ryan
Marc Sanchez
Jennifer Scappatura
Tiffany Schrader
Lori Sherman
Lori Stagnitto
Ron Stow II
Heather Strauber
Kathleen Tchorni
Allison Unruh
Dorothy Urquhart
Krista Van Ness
Eleanor Voorhees

Robert Walker
Laura Warner
Carol Wasielewski
Tara Waters
Maura Whang
Benjamin Wintner
Maryellen Zingarini
Regan Ziobro

# Selected Honors and Awards

The following list includes selected honors and awards given to Michael Graves as an individual and to the firm, Michael Graves & Associates.

American Academy in Rome: Centennial Prize, 1996; Rome Prize, 1960-1962; Brunner Fellowship, 1960

American Academy of Arts and Letters: Induction as a Member, 1991; Arnold W. Brunner Memorial Prize in Architecture, 1980

American Institute of Architects: 2001 Gold Medal

American Institute of Architects: 10 National Honor Awards, 1975–1992

AIA and American Library Association: Award of Excellence, 2001

AIA–New Jersey and other state AIA chapters: 60 design awards, 1967–2002

AIA– New Jersey: special recognition award, 1982

American Federation of Arts: Graphic design award, 1990

American Sculpture Society: Henry Hering Medal, 1986

*Architectural Digest*: "AD 100 Best Architects and Designers": 1990, 1995, 2000, 2002

Boston University: Silver Spoon Award, 1984

Chicago Athenaeum: 2 American Architecture Awards, 1999 and 2000

Chicago Athenaeum Good Design Award: 11 awards, 1997–2002

Christopher Columbus Fellowship Society, Frank Annunzio Award, 2001

Design Alliance: Most significant contribution to the design industry, 2000

Design Zentrum, Nordrhein Westfalen: Red Dot award for design quality, 2000

Downtown New Jersey, Inc.: Urban design award, 1990

Euster Merchandise Mart: Outstanding leadership in architecture and design, 1983

Friends of The Hague Citation for Improvement to the City, 1998

Fukuoka Building Contractor's Society Award, 1995

Fukuoka Urban Beautification Award: 2 awards, 1995 and 1997

GQ Magazine: Man of the Year, 1997

*House Beautiful* Magazine "Giants of Design" award, 2000

Industrial Designers Society of America: IDEA Award, 3 awards: 1999, 2001, 2003

Institute of Business Designers: 3 design awards, 1982–1990

International Furnishings & Design Assoc.: 33rd Annual Trailblazing Award, 2000

*Interiors* Magazine: 3 design awards; Designer of the Year, 1981, Hall of Fame, 1991

Japanese Society of Commercial Space Designers Design Award, 1994

Manitoga, Russel Wright Center: First Russel Wright Award, 2000

*Metropolitan Home* Magazine: Design 100 Award, 1990

National Medal of Arts, conferred by President Clinton, 1999

New Jersey Business & Industry Association: Firm Award for Achievement, 1990 and Good Neighbor Award, 2000

New Jersey Center for Visual Arts: Arts Person of the Year, 2000

New Jersey Governor's Pride Awards: Walt Whitman Creative Arts Award, 1991

Philadelphia Museum of Art: COLLAB Award, 1995

*Progressive Architecture* Magazine: 13 design awards, 1970–1989

*Progressive Architecture* Magazine: 2 furniture design awards, 1982 and 1983

Resources Council Commendations: 2 design awards, 1980 and 1982

Rhode Island School of Design and Bryant College: Success by Design Award, 2003

Tau Sigma Delta Honor Society in Architecture and the Allied Arts: The Tau Sigma Delta Gold Medal, 2003

University of Cincinnati Alumni Association: William Howard Taft Medal, 1998

# Selected Bibliography

ARCHITECTURAL MONOGRAPHS

Dobney, Stephen. *Michael Graves: Selected and Current Works*. Musgrave, Australia: Images Publishing, 1999.

Kudalis, Eric. *Michael Graves*. Minneapolis, MN: Capstone Press, 1996. [young adult textbook]

World Architecture Review Agency. *Michael Graves, Architect: World Architecture Review 96:04/05* Special Issue. Beijing, China, 1996.

Nichols, Karen, Lisa Burke, and Patrick Burke, eds. *Michael Graves: Buildings and Projects 1990–1994*. New York: Rizzoli International Publications, Inc., 1995.

Powell, Kenneth. *Graves Residence: Michael Graves*. Architecture in Detail series, London: Phaidon Press, 1995.

Brown, Theodore L. and De Vita, Maurizio, eds. *Michael Graves: Idee e projetti 1981–1991*. Milano: Electa, 1991.

Nichols, Karen Vogel, Patrick J. Burke, and Caroline Hancock, eds. *Michael Graves: Buildings and Projects 1982-1989*. New York: Princeton Architectural Press, 1990.

Wheeler, Karen Vogel, Peter Arnell, and Ted Bickford, eds. *Michael Graves: Buildings and Projects 1966–1981*. New York: Rizzoli International, 1983.

Dunster, David, ed. *Michael Graves*. London: Academy Editions, 1979.

Museum of Modern Art, New York. *Five Architects: Eisenman, Graves, Gwathmey, Hejduk, Meier*. New York: Museum of Modern Art and Oxford University Press, 1975.


PRODUCT DESIGN MONOGRAPHS

Iovine, Julie. *Compact Design Portfolio: Michael Graves*. Design Briefs series. San Francisco: Chronicle Books, 2001.

Bertsch, Georg-Christof. *Design Classics: The Water Kettle by Michael Graves*. Frankfurt am Main: Verlag form, 1997.

Buck, Alex and Matthias Vogt, eds. *Michael Graves: Designer Monographs 3*. New York: Saint Martins Press, 1994.


WRITINGS, INTERVIEWS AND ILLUSTRATIONS
BY MICHAEL GRAVES

"The Figural City." Introduction to *Town Spaces: Contemporary Interpretations in Traditional Urbanism: Krier·Kohl·Architects*, by Rob Krier. Basel: Birkhäuser, 2003.

"Henry Hornbostel." In *Invisible Giants: Fifty Americans Who Shaped the Nation but Missed the History Books*. Edited by Mark Carnes. New York: Oxford University Press, 2002.

"Michael Graves on Le Corbusier." In *Architects on Architects*. Edited by Susan Gray. New York: McGraw-Hill, 2001.

"Le Corbusier at Princeton." In *OCULUS* 63, no. 9 (May–June 2001).

"A Monumental Task." Interview by Margaret Warner. *NewsHour with Jim Lehrer* (2 March 1999).

Cover illustration. *Italy in Mind*. Edited by Alice Leccese Powers. New York: Vintage Books, a division of Random House, Inc., 1997.

"Architecture of the Michael C. Carlos Museum." In *Handbook*. Atlanta, GA: Michael C. Carlos Museum, Emory University, 1996.

"Commentary by Michael Graves." Preface to *World Architecture Review: Michael Graves*, April/May 1996.

"Humana Building a Louisville." *Paesaggio urbano*, July–October 1996.

"Sketches – An interview with Michael Graves." Edited by Alex Buck and Mathias Vogt. *Michael Graves: Designer Monographs 3*. Berlin: Ernst & Sohn, 1994.

"Michael Graves." Interview by Stanley Collyer. *Competitions*, Winter 1994.

Illustrations for *Mr. Chas and Lisa Sue Meet the Pandas*, by Fran Lebowitz. New York: Alfred A. Knopf, Inc., 1994.

"Michael Graves." Interview by Gordon Simmons. *Practices: Journal of the Center for the Study of the Practice of Architecture* (University of Cincinnati) 2 (Spring 1993).

"A Conversation with Michael Graves." Interview by John R. Kirk. *Modulus: The Architectural Review of the University of Virginia*. New York: Princeton Architectural Press, 1989.

"Has Post-modernism reached its limit?" *Architectural Digest Supplement*, April 1988.

"Graves/Schmidt: Competition Statement." In *Art + architecture + landscape: The Clos Pegase Design Competition*. San Francisco, CA: San Francisco Museum of Modern Art, 1985.

Illustrations for *The Great Gatsby*, by F. Scott Fitgerald. San Francisco: The Arion Press, 1984.

"A Case for Figurative Architecture." In *Michael Graves: Buildings and Projects 1966–1981*. Edited by Karen Vogel Nichols, Patrick J. Burke and Caroline Hancock. New York: Rizzoli International Publications, Inc., 1983.

"Ritual Themes in Architecture." *The Princeton Journal*, 1983.

"Michael Graves on Michael Graves." *GA Document*, 1983.

"Representation." In *Representation and Architecture*. Edited by Omer Akin and Eleanor F. Weinel. Information Dynamics, 1982.

"Le Corbusier's Drawn References." In *Le Corbusier: Selected Drawings*. London: Academy Editions, 1981.

"Michael Graves." In *Architectural Drawing: The Art and the Process*. Gerald Allen and Richard Oliver, editors. New York: Whitney Library of Design, 1981.

"The Wageman House and the Crooks House." In *Idea as Model*. New York, Institute for Architecture and Urban Studies: Rizzoli International Publications, Inc., 1981.

"Michael Graves." In *Speaking a New Classicism: American Architecture Now*. Smith College Museum of Art, 1981.

"Porta Maggiore." In *Roma Interrotta Incontri Internazionale d'Arte*. Rome, 1978.

"Toward Reading an Architecture." Interview by Douglas Ely. *Nassau Literary Review*, Princeton University, Spring 1978.

"Thought Models." *Great Models*, North Carolina State School of Design, Fall 1978.

"Referential Drawings." *Journal of Architectural Education*, September 1978.

"The Necessity of Drawing: Tangible Speculation." *Architectural Design*, June 1977.

"The Swedish Connection." *Journal of Architectural Education*, September 1975.


ARTICLES

Pugh, Clifford. "Rice refreshed: New campus buildings expand on tradition." *Houston Chronicle*, 10 March 2003. [Rice University North College residence halls]

Rich, Motoko. "Michael Graves Enters his Post-Teapot Phase." *Wall Street Journal*, 26 March 2003. [Target Pavilions]

Margolies, Jane. "Good Design Means Business." *House Beautiful*. Giants of Design issue, June 2003. [Product design]

Goldberger, Paul. "Cincinnati Synthesis: Turning Disparate Design Elements into a Unified Whole." *Architectural Digest*, April 2001. [Residence at Indian Hill]

Ivy, Robert. "Michael Graves: The Road to Gold." *Architectural Record*, May 2001. [Cover: AIA Gold Medal]

Davidson, Cynthia. "Michael Graves: O'Reilly Theater, Pittsburgh." *Architecture*, May 2001.

Catinella, Rita. "Michael Graves: Man of the House." *Architectural Record*, April 2000. [Products design]

Clines, Francis X. "A Washington Cover-Up With Aesthetic Appeal." *New York Times*, 17 January 2000. [Washington Monument Restoration Scaffolding]

Gibney, Frank, Jr. and Belinda Luscombe. "The Redesigning of America." *Time Magazine*, 20 March 2000.

Pittel, Christine. "Giants of Design: An Intimate Look at Seven Who Changed Our World; Michael Graves, Product Design." *House Beautiful*, June 2000.

Goldberger, Paul. "Architecture: Malibu Composition: A Play of Grids and Circles Embraces its Oceanfront Site." *Architectural Digest*, October 2000. [Malibu Beach House]

Naegele, Daniel. "We Dig Graves – All Sizes." *Harvard Design Magazine*, Fall 2000.

Schmertz, Mildred F. "Egyptian Mirage: Michael Graves' Sheraton Miramar Rises on the Red Sea." Photography by Erhard Pfeiffer, *Architectural Digest*, January 1999. [The Miramar Hotel, El Gouna Egypt]

Forgey, Benjamin. "The Monument's New Winter Coat: Temporary Transformation of Obelisk Is Quite a Treat." *The Washington Post* Style section, 23 January 1999. [Washington Monument Restoration Scaffolding]

Sogg, Daniel. "Classic Harmony: Architect Michael Graves and His Collections." *Art & Antiques*, April 1999. [Graves Residence - The Warehouse]

Kamin, Blair. "A D.C. '10': Elegant scaffolding on Washington Monument captivates capital city." *Chicago Tribune Arts & Entertainment*, 4 July 1999.

Goldberger, Paul, with photograph by Todd Eberle. "Postmodern Pillar." Showcase section, *The New Yorker*, 4 October 1999 [Washington Monument Restoration Scaffolding]

Curtis, Eleanor. "Intonaco: Michael Graves in Egitto: Miramar Hotel." *Abitare*, February 1998. [The Miramar Hotel, El Gouna Egypt]

Russell, John. "Architect Gives a Library Space to Read and Dream." *New York Times*, 4 November 1998. [The French Institute Library]

Rozhon, Tracie. "Michael Graves: The Prince of Princeton." *Graphis 312*, Volume 53 (November/December 1997).

Allen, Jenny. "The 1996 LIFE Dream House." *LIFE*, May 1996.

Brown, Patricia L. "At Home with Michael Graves: How the Pearl Designed his Oyster." *New York Times*, 14 March 1996. [Graves Residence – The Warehouse]

Goldberger, Paul. "A Little Book That Led Five Men to Fame." *New York Times*, 11 February 1996. [retrospective look at Five Architects]

Goldsmith, Barbara. "Architecture: The American Academy's Rare Book Room: A Michael Graves Design Enhances Preservation in Rome." *Architectural Digest*, December 1996.

Hoyt, Charles. "Hyatt Regency Hotel." *Architectural Record*, October 1996. [Hyatt Regency Hotel, Fukuoka, Japan]

Hoyt, Charles. "Joining Hands to Connect a Campus." *Architectural Record*, July 1996. [University of Cincinnati Engineering Research Center]

Prisant, Carol. "Graves' New World." *World of Interiors*, May 1995. [Graves Residence – The Warehouse]

Fukuwatari, Isao. "The Tajima Building" (*in Japanese*). *Shinkenchiku*, July 1994. [Tajima Office Building, Tokyo, Japan]

Goldberger, Paul. "Rural Revisited: Working Wonders on a New Jersey Farm Property." *Architectural Digest*, May 1994. [Dairy Barn Renovation, NJ]

Goldberger, Paul. "A Remembrance of Visions Pure and Elegant." *New York Times*, 3 January 1993. [on lecture: "Five Architects 20 Years Later"]

Hamano, Yasuhiro. "Onjuku Town Hall and Health Center." *Shinkenchiku*, July 1993. [Article in Japanese on Onjuku Civic Center]

Russell, Beverly. "The Hotel New York." *Interiors*, May 1992. [Hotel New York: Disneyland Park – Paris]

"Momochi District Apartment Building." *Architektur + Wettbewerbe*, September 1991.

Sutro, Dirk. "Classical Animation." *Architecture*, June 1991. [Team Disney Building, Burbank, CA]

Branch, Mark Alden. "Design Feature: Fish Story." *Progressive Architecture*, October 1990. [Walt Disney World® Swan and Dolphin Hotels]

Branch, Mark Alden. "Story Time." *Progressive Architecture*, March 1990. [Walt Disney World Swan® and Dolphin Hotels]

Lavin, Sylvia. "Michael Graves, Architect: Growth and Diversity." *Progressive Architecture*, March 1990.

Brown, Patricia L. "Disney Deco." *New York Times* Magazine, 8 April 1990. [Team Disney Building, Burbank, CA]

Goldberger, Paul. "And Now, an Architectural Kingdom." *New York Times* Magazine, 8 April 1990. [Walt Disney World® Swan and Dolphin Hotels]

Goldberger, Paul. "Raising the Architectural Ante in California." *New York Times*, 14 October 1990. [The Aventine Hotel and Business Center, La Jolla, CA]

Papademetriou, Peter. "Four Not-so-easy Pieces." *Progressive Architecture*, March 1990. [The Newark Museum]

Schreiner, Judy. "Irrepressible Michael Graves." *Engineering News Record*, 6 September 1990.

Stein, Karen D. "Gravesian Images." *Architectural Record*, February 1990. [Cover: Crown American Headquarters, Johnstown, PA]

Glueck, Grace. "A 'Yellow Brick Road' Brightens a Museum." *New York Times*, 12 November 1989. [The Newark Museum]

Pastier, John. "An Intimate Sequence of Spaces." *Architecture*, December 1989. [San Juan Capistrano Library]

Byron, Elizabeth S. "The Prince of Princeton." *HG*, July 1988.

Viladas, Pilar. "Mickey the Talent Scout." *Progressive Architecture*, June 1988. [Disney projects]

Filler, Martin. "A Shrine to Wine." *House & Garden*, September 1987. [Clos Pegase Winery, Calistoga, CA]

Giovannini, Joseph. "Designers' Showrooms That Reflect Architectural Trends." *New York Times*, 29 January 1987. [Sunar Showrooms]

Stein, Karen D. "On the Waterfront." *Architectural Record*, October 1986. [Riverbend Music Center for Cincinnati Symphony Orchestra]

Gandee, Charles K. "Humana." *Architectural Record*, August 1985. [The Humana Building, Louisville, KY]

Viladas, Pilar. "Full Circle." *Progressive Architecture*, September 1985. [Emory University Michael C. Carlos Museum of Art and Archaeology]

Jordy, William H. "Aedicular Modern: The Architecture of Michael Graves." *New Criterion*, October 1983.

Goldberger, Paul. "Architecture of a Different Color." *New York Times Magazine*, 10 October 1982.

Gandee, Charles. "Sunar Houston: The Allusive Language of Michael Graves." *Architectural Record*, June 1980.

Filler, Martin. "Better and Better." *Progressive Architecture*, September 1979. [Sunar Showrooms, Los Angeles and Chicago]

Filler, Martin. "Grand Illusions." *Progressive Architecture*, June 1979. [Sunar Showroom, New York City]

"Five on Five." *Architectural Forum*, May 1973. ["Stompin' at the Savoy" by Robert A.M. Stern; "Machines in the Garden" by Jacquelin Robertson; "In Similar States of Undress" by Charles Moore; "The Lurking American Legacy" by Allan Greenberg; "The Discreet Charm of the Bourgeoisie" by Romaldo Giurgola]

BOOKS

*US Design 1975–2000*. New York: Prestel Verlag in association with the Denver Art Museum, 2002.

Fentriss, Curtis W. *Civic Builders*. New York: John Wiley & Sons, 2002.

Futagawa, Yukio. "Plocek House, Warren, New Jersey, USA." *GA Houses Special, Masterpieces 1971–2000 Edition*. Tokyo: A.D.A. Editor Tokyo, Ltd., 2002.

Gronin, Pierrette. *Cyberculture et objects de design industriel*. Laval, Canada: Les Presses de l'Université Laval, Fall 2000.

"Michael Graves & Associates." *Architects of the New Millennium*. Mulgrave, Australia: Images Publishing, 2000.

Powell, Kenneth. "Michael Graves Architect." In *Architecture Reborn: The Conversion and Reconstruction of Old Buildings*. London: Laurence King Publishing, May 1999.

Liu Erming/Yi Feng. *International Architects in China*. Beijing: China Planning Press, 1999.

Wiseman, Carter. *Shaping A Nation*. New York City: W.W. Norton & Company, Inc., 1999.

Byars, Mel and Arlette Barré-Despond. *Cent Objets: Un Siècle de Design*. Les Editions de l'Amateur, 1999.

Pearman, Hugh. *Contemporary World Architecture*. London: Phaidon Press Limited, 1998.

Bertsch, Georg Christof. *The Water Kettle by Michael Graves*. Frankfurt am Main: Design-Klassiker Verlag form, 1997.

Riewoldt, Otto. *Intelligent Spaces: Architecture for the Information Age*. London: Laurence King Publishing, 1997.

Myerson, Jeremy. "The Denver Central Library." *New Public Architecture*. London: Laurence King Publishing, 1996.

Lebowitz, Fran. "The Warehouse." In *Building Sights*. Edited by Ruth Rosenthal and Maggie Toy (100–105). London: Academy Editions, 1995.

University of Maryland. *Five Architects: Twenty Years Later*. Introduction by Steven W. Hurtt. College Park: University of Maryland, 1992.

Spencer, Dorothy. *Total Design: Objects by Architects*. San Francisco: Chronicle Books, 1991.

Papadakis, Dr. Andreas C., ed. A.D. (*Architectural Design*) Profile No. 88: "*Post-Modernism on Trial*." London: Academy Group Ltd, 1990. [Walt Disney World® Dolphin and Swan Hotels (cover), Newark Museum]

Papadakis, Andreas and Watson, Harriet, eds. *New Classicism: Omnibus Volume*. New York: Rizzoli International Publications and London: Academy Editions, 1990.

Tapert, Annette. *Swid Powell: Objects by Architects*. New York: Rizzoli International Publications, Inc., 1990.

Collins, Michael and Andreas Papadakis. *Post Modern Design*. New York: Rizzoli International Publications, Inc., 1989.

Shoshkes, Ellen. *The Design Process*. New York: Whitney Library of Design, 1989.

Fleischmann, Melanie. *In the Neoclassic Style*. New York: Thames and Hudson, 1988.

Papadakis, Dr. Andreas C. AD (*Architectural Design*) Vol 58 No 1/2 – 1988; "*Michael Graves: Two Recent Projects*." London: Academy Group Ltd., 1988. [Clos Pegase Winery & WVU Alumni Center]

Merkel, Jayne. *Michael Graves and the Riverbend Music Center*. Cincinnati: Contemporary Arts Center, 1987.

Stephens, Suzanne, et al., eds. *Building the New Museum*. New York: The Architectural League of New York, 1986.

Poling, Clark V. *Henry Hornbostel/Michael Graves*. Atlanta: Emory University Museum of Art and Archaeology, 1985.

*GA Document 10*, Tokyo: May, 1984. [Cincinnati Symphony Summer Pavilion; The Humana Building; San Juan Capistrano Public Library (cover); Liberty State Park Environmental Education Center; The Portland Building; others.]

Jencks, Charles. *The Language of Post-Modern Architecture*, Fourth Revised Enlarged Edition. London: Academy Editions, London, 1984.

Jencks, Charles. *Kings of Infinite Space: Michael Graves and Frank Lloyd Wright*. London: Academy Editions, 1984.

Arnell, Peter and Ted Bickford eds. *A Tower for Louisville: The Humana Competition*, New York: Rizzoli International Publications, Inc., 1982.

"Michael Graves: Sunar." *GA Document 10*, Tokyo: 1982.

Jensen, Robert, and Patricia Conway. *Ornamentalism: The Return of Decorativeness in Modern Design and Art*. New York: C.N. Potter, 1982.

Turner, Judith. *Judith Turner Photographs Five Architects*. New York: Rizzoli International Publications, Inc., 1980.

Emanuel, Muriel. *Contemporary Architects*. Edited with Architectural Consultant Dennis Sharp. New York: St. Martin's Press, 1980.

Cerruti, Marisa, ed. *Roma interrotta*. Rome: 1978.

Gebhard, David, and Deborah Nevins. *200 Years of American Architectural Drawing*. New York: Whitney Library of Design for the Architectural League of New York and The American Federation of Arts, 1977.

Jencks, Charles. *The Language of Post Modern Architecture*. London: Academy Editions, 1977.

Stern, Robert A.M. *New Directions in American Architecture*. New York: George Braziller, 1977.

# Photography Credits

1500 Ocean Drive, 44-47: ©Steven Brooke Studio

Astrid Park Plaza Hotel, 24–27: ©Luc Polfliet, except 25 top, 26 bottom, MGA

Castalia, 28–33: ©Daria Scagliola and Stijn Brakkee

Cedar Gables, 208–213: ©Susan Gilmore

Charles E. Beatley, Jr. Central Library, 116–119: ©Eric Taylor Photography

Disney's Garden Pavilion, 43: ©William Taylor/Taylor Photo; with permission of The Walt Disney Company

El Gouna Golf Hotel and Club, 134–145: ©John Donat

Elephant Fountain at Target House, 227: courtesy of Target House

Famille-Tsukishima, 250–251: courtesy of Maeda Corporation

Fortis AG Headquarters, 132–133: ©Luc Polfliet, except exterior image, MGA

Golf Villas, 146–149: ©John Donat, except 148 top, MGA

House at Coolidge Point, 50–55: ©John Bellenis Photography

House at Indian Hill, 106–113: Scott Frances (Photographs on pages 109 and 112, courtesy of Architectural Digest, ©2001 Condé Nast Publications, Inc.)

Hyatt Regency Hotel, 82–89: ©John Donat, except 88, Erhard Pfeiffer (Photograph courtesy Architectural Digest ©1999 Condé Nast Publications, Inc. This image was photographed by Erhard Pfeiffer at a different location, the Miramar Hotel in El Gouna, a companion project for the same developer. It shows a guestroom design that was replicated at the Hyatt Regency Hotel in Taba Heights.)

Indianapolis Art Center, 22–23: ©William Taylor/Taylor Photo

International Finance Corporation Headquarters, 14–19: ©Andrew Lautman/Lautman Photography

Lake Hills Country Club, 98–101: ©Seung Hoon Yum

Laurel Hall, New Jersey Institute of Technology, 66–67: ©William Taylor/Taylor Photo

Library of the French Institute/Alliance Française, 102–103: ©Cervin Robinson

LIFE Magazine Dream House, 104–105: cover image courtesy of LIFE Magazine

Main Library of Topeka and Shawnee County, 68–71: ©Douglas Kahn Photography

Martel, Jones and Brown Colleges, Rice University, 194–203: ©Jud Haggard Photography

Miele Americas Headquarters, 92–95: ©William Taylor/Taylor Photo

Miramar Resort Hotel, 56–63: ©Daniel Aubry, except 62 top, Erhard Pfeiffer (Photograph courtesy of Architectural Digest, ©1999, Condé Nast Publications, Inc.) and 63, ©John Donat

Mixed-use Building, 160–161: courtesy of Fukuoka Jisho Co.

Museum of the Shenandoah Valley, 242–245: 245 bottom courtesy of Glen Burnie and the Museum of the Shenandoah Valley

NCAA Headquarters and Hall of Champions, 126–131: 126–127, 129 top, ©William Taylor/ Taylor; 130, 131, ©Greg Murphey

Nexus Momochi Residential Tower, 34–35: courtesy of Maeda Corporation

North Hall, Drexel University, 156–159: ©Matt Wargo

NovaCare Complex, Philadelphia Eagles Training Center, 220–223: ©Matt Wargo

O'Grady Library, Saint Martin's College, 168–169: ©Doug Walker

One Port Center, 48–49: ©Matt Wargo

O'Reilly Theater, 72–79: ©Ed Massery, except 75 top, 79, ©Barney Taxel

Private Offices, 254–257: ©Robert Lautman/Lautman Photography

St. Mary's Church, 188–191: ©Steven Brooke Studio

Taiwan National Museum of Pre-History, 36–37: 40 top, ©Jeffrey Cheng; 40 bottom, 41, ©Peter Mauss/ESTO

Target Stage at Harriet Island Park, 226: courtesy of Rafferty Rafferty Tollefson Architects

The Impala, 170–173: ©Norman McGrath, except 173 bottom, MGA

Uffelman Country House, 120–123: ©George Kopp Photography

United States Post Office, 42: ©William Taylor/Taylor Photo; with permission of The Walt Disney Company

Washington Monument Restoration, 176–179: ©Robert Lautman/Lautman Photography

Watch Technicum, 228-231: ©Larry Lefever